"Every day I receive heart-breaking letters and phone calls from people who have lost all hope because they have been diagnosed with cancer. Frightened, helpless and scared, they—and their families—often have resigned themselves to a difficult and painful death. They should not! With surrender to God through sincere prayer, I have seen literally thousands of people conquer cancer. That is what this wonderful and inspiring book is all about. *The Healing Power of Prayer* is more than a book about positive thinking. It is a roadmap to positive living. This work inspires, instructs and gives hope. In that sense, it truly heals. *The Healing Power of Prayer* should be required reading for anyone interested in health enhancement and life enrichment. I predict this book will become a classic for people going through illness . . . a true 'gift with a lift' to the human spirit."

—Greg Anderson, founding chairman,
Cancer Recovery Foundation International;
author of *The Cancer Conqueror and Cancer: 50 Essential Things to Do*

"Many of us have experienced the power of prayer to make a difference in our lives. Nevertheless, our prayers for healing do not seem to be always answered. These two authors have written a most helpful book, offering concrete ways in which God's healing power can be appropriated. It is sure to increase your faith and strengthen your prayer life."

—Dr. Bruce Larson, pastor emeritus,
University Presbyterian Church, Seattle, Washington

"*The Healing Power of Prayer* brings together the expertise of two established authors—a clergyman and a physician and leading research scholar. Together they present an informative, readable and practical work on the effects of religion and prayer on stress, health and healing. With a particular focus on the Christian tradition, they have coupled scholarship, experience and personal reflection to produce a work that is unique among its kind. It should find an important place in the library of clinicians, clergy and others who are interested in the efficacy of prayer."

—Margaret M. Poloma, Ph.D., University of Akron, author of
(together with George H. Gallup, Jr.) *Varieties of Prayer*

"Chester Tolson and Harold Koenig offer convincing reason and rationale to something we have intuitively known for years, that there is a definite connection between prayer and healing. Their fresh, insightful approach to the subject of prayer also shows the tremendous influence of prayer on a healthy, stress-free lifestyle. Complete with guidance to develop a more effective prayer life, it's a book on prayer we have all been waiting for!"

—Dr. Ray Cotton, senior pastor,
New Hope Community Church, Portland, Oregon

"At last! An excellent work that brings faith and science together in a way both compelling and readable. Drs. Tolson and Koenig are men of prayer, and their holistic approach to the unity of body, mind, and spirit encourages us all to believe that prayer can and does, indeed, make us whole and holy. In a day when scientific research into the power of healing prayer is literally exploding, this book gives us all an accessible, friendly, down-to-earth entry into this topic. Chapters on the interweaving of faith, grace, the mind, and serenity are worth reading again and again. With this book, Drs. Tolson and Koenig have given the Christian faith community a gift and a blessing. I will surely recommend it to members of my congregation."

—Rev. C. Lou Martin, pastor,
The Catholic Faith Community of St. Anthony of Padua
& Most Precious Blood, Baltimore, Maryland

"A truly wonderful book demonstrating the power of prayer in helping us to live more balanced and effective daily lives. The authors' personal testimonies to prayer's efficacy as well as the powerful stories of others healings have once more convicted me that prayer is not merely a preparation for ministry—it is our ministry! Prayer works! It positively changes things because, through it, God changes us!"

—Rev. Michael Ward, senior pastor,
Central United Church, Calgary, Alberta, Canada

"In 1947 God's Spirit awakened me! Yet in prayer I was frustrated and discouraged, but determined. Slowly they became clear—the dynamics of effective prayer. Now I have discovered them afresh in *The Healing Power of Prayer*."

—Louis H. Evans, pastor emeritus,
National Presbyterian Church, Washington, D.C.

"This book could not be more timely. We are becoming increasingly more aware of how the body, mind, and spirit work together in keeping us healthy. Prayer is an important part of the healing process. This book explores how prayer works and you may use it in your own lives. I recommend you read it carefully."

—Dr. Robert H. Schuller, founding pastor, Crystal Cathedral Ministries, Garden Grove, California

"With deep knowledge born from study, experience and active prayer, the Rev. Dr. Chet Tolson and Dr. Harold Koenig have combined their extraordinary ability to create an influential and important guide to help us further connect our lives and the spiritual life. 'Prayer is medicine for the soul!' state the authors. It is true! It speeds recovery in illness, it connects our bodies, minds, and psyches to God's great presence, it brings us into a closer relationship with the God and Father of our Lord, Jesus Christ. As a parish pastor who has seen the power of prayer at work, *The Healing Power of Prayer* captures precisely what members of my church can find most beneficial in their daily lives. I look forward to sharing it with my congregation and colleagues."

—Steven E. Berry, D.D., D. Min., pastor, "The Meetinghouse," Manchester, Vermont

"A rich banquet of clinical, pastoral, and personal experience that highlights the healing power of prayer and nourishes the mind, body, and soul."

—Dale A. Matthews, M.D., author of *The Faith Factor: Proof of the Healing Power of Prayer*

"I am persuaded that the authors of this book, *The Healing Power of Prayer*, present a positive and constructive view of God's plan for a balanced view of Christian living. As a Pentecostal pastor for over forty years, I would highly recommend it to the world of full Gospel believers."

—Dr. Fulton W. Buntain, senior pastor, Life Center, Tacoma, Washington

"Bringing together a rich assortment of credentials and life experiences, Tolson and Koenig masterfully blend faith and medicine. In an age when there is such a great hunger for the spiritual, it is helpful to see how the spiritual and the physical work together in harmony. This book is a must read for people in the helping professions."

—Jim Capps, senior pastor, Southport Presbyterian Church

THE
HEALING
POWER
of
PRAYER

THE
HEALING
POWER
of
PRAYER

The Surprising Connection
between Prayer and Your Health

CHESTER L. TOLSON, PH.D.
&
HAROLD G. KOENIG, M.D.

A Division of Baker Book House Co
Grand Rapids, Michigan 49516

*T*he authors dedicate this book to their wives, who also believe in the power of prayer and have encouraged them in writing the book:

Carol Ann Tolson
Charmin Marie Koenig

We also dedicate this book to people everywhere who pray faithfully and believe in prayer's healing power.

We give special thanks to Kathleen Tolson for bringing all the drafts together into a manuscript for the publisher.

We also give special thanks to Vicki Crumpton, senior acquisitions editor for Baker Books, whose input in creating this book and helpful suggestions for its content were most valuable.

Contents

FOREWORD

A growing number of Americans (nine in ten in the latest audit) pray and believe in the power of prayer. Eight in ten believe that miracles can happen today. A remarkable three persons in ten report instances of a profound healing of a physical, emotional, or spiritual nature. This proportion projects to sixty million adults.

The American people have consistently told pollsters over the last fifty years that prayer brings them many positive results, including a deep feeling of well-being, strength, and courage, and a sense of the presence of God. Yet while Americans are a praying population, it was not until the final decades of the twentieth century that the scientific community and medical professionals began in earnest to study this fundamental fact about human life.

Many who pray seek a closer link between the medical and spiritual worlds. For example, while presently only 6 percent of persons interviewed nationally indicate that their doctors pray for them at times of serious illness, eight times this proportion would like them to do so. Among those who experienced a doctor praying with them, as many as 93 percent think the doctor's prayer helped them with their medical problems. In addition, most (97 percent) believe the prayers helped them recover.

Most who pray, furthermore, would like to deepen their prayer lives. Surveys suggest that the prayer life of Americans tends to be undeveloped and undernourished. Significant numbers feel that their churches could better serve them by helping them to develop and strengthen the role of prayer in their daily lives.

Even among those most dedicated to prayer, persistent questions predictably arise: Why does prayer seem to work in some cases but not others? Is God really listening? Does prayer really help to bring about healing of the body and the mind? How can one learn to accept prayer in the context of God's eternal love and oversight?

The Healing Power of Prayer is making a timely appearance and sheds new light on these basic questions. It is authored by two men who speak from a wealth of experience in their respective disciplines, each man a dedicated believer in the power of prayer.

Dr. Harold Koenig, director of Duke University's Center for the Study of Religion/Spirituality and Health, is a pioneer in his field, and for the last quarter-century he has, through his own studies and the studies of others, brought exciting new findings to light showing the relationship of prayer to health.

He is teamed with Dr. Chester Tolson, who brings his many years of experience as a pastor and teacher to this book. This dual authorship is a real plus for the reader since it links the scientific world to the spiritual world and provides practical suggestions on how one can live a deeper and ongoing life of prayer.

Drs. Koenig and Tolson cover many aspects of prayer, including the types of prayer, grace and prayer, and the power of praying together. This last topic, covered in the final chapter of the book, has particular meaning for me. My wife and I have been members of small Bible study and prayer groups for the last twenty years and can testify to the power of praying in a group—we have seen many miracles in terms of healed relationships and in many other ways.

The Healing Power of Prayer brings the reader up to date on findings from numerous studies that reveal the wide range of health benefits, both of mind and body, that can be linked to prayer, thus undergirding what people presently believe on the basis of intuition or faith. The authors deduce from studies that "faith and belief in God activate the physiological processes in the body—the immune system, the hormone system, and the circulatory system—to speed healing and recovery."

Direct supernatural intervention is not ruled out. The authors point out that there are many healings for which no medical explanation is possible. Particularly fascinating is their speculation that God, in such miraculous healings, may be breaking through the established order of creation by altering the course of nature at the atomic or subatomic level in a way that is undetectable to modern medical science. And we need to remember, the authors note, that God exists outside time and space and can make alterations in nature in such ways that cannot be observed by people living today.

Koenig and Tolson, very importantly, remind us that there are numerous forces that are at work during healing experiences—medicines and drugs; medical technology; surgery; faith; caregiving, and prayer. These are, they write, "gifts from God to help us with the healing process."

Readers who are intent on informing and deepening their prayer lives will find this book to be of great help. Counselors in many fields will discover that *The Healing Power of Prayer* belongs among the most important books on their desks.

From a personal point of view, this book will be very helpful to me as a member of the healing ministry team at my church and as a hospital caller. And as a "cancer survivor" myself, I find *The Healing Power of Prayer* to be an enlightening and profoundly reassuring book.

This book offers many important insights and observations. One that readily comes to mind is this: that healing should not be categorized as either strictly due to medicine or strictly due to faith—"All healing is divine, all healing requires faith, and all healing is miraculous in that people are made whole again."

George Gallup, Jr.

INTRODUCTION

In 1962 Rev. Chester L. Tolson, then pastor of the Village Presbyterian Church in Rancho Santa Fe, California, coauthored the book *Peace and Power through Prayer* with Clarence William Lieb, M.D. Dr. Lieb had been the private physician of the late Rev. Norman Vincent Peale in New York. He was also one of the founders, with Dr. Peale, of the American Foundation of Religion and Psychiatry. It was Dr. Peale who encouraged the writing and publication of that book and wrote the introduction. He wrote about the joint effort of a physician and a clergyman on the subject of prayer. Dr. Peale was at the time the senior pastor of the Marble Collegiate Church in New York City and had written the best-seller *The Power of Positive Thinking* ten years before. Being a pastor, and having family in the medical profession, he had great interest in and insight on how prayer is a factor in healing.

In his introduction, Dr. Peale pointed out that this "collaboration of physician and minister was a bridge builder between these two old and respected professions of medicine and ministry."[1] Furthermore, he noted how in

> recent years, physicians and pastors have worked in even closer cooperation, based, no doubt, upon the modern recognition that the whole man must be considered in the healing process, that

disease may be induced from fractures within the soul, no less than infections by germ transmission. Many modern doctors acknowledge that mental health is inseparably related to physical well being. That many people are draining back into their bodies the diseased thoughts of their minds is a very well known phenomenon. Thus, cures are increasingly related to healthy states of mind, which in turn lead to a cleansed condition of the soul.[2]

In the book *Peace and Power through Prayer,* Tolson and Lieb developed a section on prayer and health. They said that since the mind affects the body and prayer can affect the mind, so prayer can affect the body. "Therefore, prayer can be a significant factor in the preservation of health and in the prevention of disease."[3] They went on to suggest that specific physiological processes in the body might be favorably affected by the calming influence of prayer.

Moreover, they said, "Prayer might aid in the production of antibodies in combating diseases."[4] At that time, they said that early studies were underway to establish the relationship between stress and the immune system. In the laboratory, two groups of mice were infected with the same amount of destructive germs. One group of infected mice was placed in a "free-run" environment, and the other group was put in a maze. The mice that were stressed out in the confusion of the maze had a much slower recuperative period if they survived. The mice in the free-run setting were much more likely to fully recover. That simple test illustrated that the mice under stress apparently could not mount an immune response to fight off the infection as well as could the mice that were not under stress. Studies at that same time also found a correlation between stress and health in humans. Today, since prayer may be a factor in reducing stress, we also thought that prayer might assist in physical healing.

Since that time, much scientific research has been done that has corroborated the hypothesis that thoughts and feelings can influence the cardiovascular and immune systems. In over seventy medical schools across the United States today, medical students are taught about the mind, body, and spirit relationship and its implications for human health. Over the past forty years, many best-selling books have been written on the theme that how we think may influence our health. Names like Norman Cousins, Bernie Seigel, and Carl Simonton, to name a few, have been among the popular spokespersons in this area.

A whole new discipline called "psychoneuroimmunology," shortened to PNI, has been developed to address the relationship of the mind to the body. Over the past half-century, much research has linked what goes on in the brain to health and illness in other parts of the body. According to a recent *Newsweek* article titled "God and the Brain," we may be "wired" for God.[5]

Over the past ten years, scientists have also examined the effects of religious beliefs and practices such as prayer on physical and mental health and well-being. I have been fortunate to help contribute to this area of research as director of Duke University's Center for the Study of Religion/Spirituality and Health. As a physician, biostatistician, and associate professor of psychiatry and medicine at Duke University Medical Center, I have helped to conduct over twenty-five research studies exploring the link between religion and health. My colleagues and I recently compiled much of the research done on this topic over the past one hundred years in the *Handbook of Religion and Health* (Oxford University Press, 2001). Over five hundred studies have now documented correlations between religious practices like prayer and better health. I have also seen the powerful effects of faith in the lives of my patients, and what a tremendous difference prayer has made in their healing—physical, emotional, social, and spiritual. There is power in prayer—there is little doubt about that.

I read the book *Peace and Power through Prayer* written by my friend Chet Tolson and Dr. Lieb. Dr. Lieb has been deceased for several years. Chet and I decided after a number of face-to-face meetings, correspondence by mail and e-mail, and many telephone calls that it was time to write a new book on the subject of stress, religion, and health to bring the discoveries of recent years to light.

Prayer is very important in my own life. Every day I take time to pray, usually in the morning after I wake up. Throughout the day as I encounter difficulties or stresses or internal struggles, I talk with God about it. For me, prayer begins with adoration and worship. I recognize who God is—the creator of everything that has ever been and that ever will be; the person who first thought of me and brought me into being; the one who, at the moment of my death, I will leap toward and whose strong and loving arms will catch me. Next, I recognize who I am. I confess all of the selfish decisions, thoughts, and strivings that have hurt others. I confess pride, arrogance, and lack of kindness and compassion. I confess worry over things that really don't matter. I confess my lack of attention to God and to the things of God during the day. Then I express thanks. I have been blessed with physical and mental health, a comfortable house, plenty of food, a loving wife and two beautiful children, other caring family members, friends and colleagues, a fulfilling and fun job, freedom in the greatest nation in the world, and, more than anything, faith in and a relationship with a loving God who gives my life purpose and direction. Finally, I ask God for things. I ask him to protect the physical and emotional health of my mother, who must care for my ailing father, completely immobilized by a massive stroke, locked in his body unable to speak or even swallow. I ask him to stay by my father's side and never leave him for an instant. I ask for blessings for my friends and coworkers and for the many for whom I have promised to pray. I ask for greater faith and trust so that I would not worry about the present or the future. Then I listen. It's God's turn to talk. As a five-year-old boy secretly confided in his grandfather one day, "When I go to bed at night and it gets really dark and really quiet in my room, if I hold my breath, lay very still and listen carefully, I hear Jesus talking." The little boy could hear Jesus talking. That small, quiet voice in the night. What a beautiful illustration describing the time to be quiet and silent in prayer, listening for God's voice. Why pray? For me, it is to spend time with the closest friend I will ever have here in this life and in the next.

While the book is about prayer and its healing potential for mental and physical illness, it is not restricted to health matters alone. It is a book about prayer. It addresses the whole subject of prayer: what it is, how to pray, what happens when we pray, and how to pray more effectively when we have a visit with God.

Harold. G. Koenig, M.D.

1

PRAYER POWER

At 10:03 A.M. on Thursday, March 14, 2002, my heart stopped beating. I (Chet) was lying on the table in the catheterization lab undergoing angioplasty. The procedure seemed to be going along well. I was awake and could hear the conversations of the medical team. As they worked, I was praying and conversing with God. Suddenly I felt severe chest pains, and the doctor in charge hit my chest hard with his fists. I knew I was in trouble. I could hear the orders being given to inject medication through the IV line in my arm and to place the defibrillation paddles on my chest to shock my heart back into normal rhythm. The team of doctors, nurses, and technicians were busy doing many things to restore me to life.

I was busy praying. A few seconds before it would have been "too late," my heart started to beat again. At this most stressful moment of my life, I was not in control of what was happening to my own body. Nevertheless, I was linked to God for my healing through the power of prayer. Prayer has been an important part of daily life throughout most of my life. So it is natural for me to pray about everything happening in my life. At this moment of physical crisis, therefore, it was comfortable for me to pray.

This personal story brings together the numerous forces at work during my healing experience. They included:

- Medicines and drugs
- Medical technology
- Surgery
- Attitude
- Faith
- Caregiving
- Prayer

All of these elements working together create healing. Each is like a small arc that when placed end to end and united with the other arcs, makes a person well. We might call this "arc healing" in that each healing agent has a key role in creating this dynamic circle of wellness.

Health and Humanity

Humanity is subject to illness. Beginning with the earliest records of human life, evidence exists that humans have sought wellness:

- 6000 B.C.—Artifacts indicate that illness was treated as evil spirits and demon possession.
- 5000 B.C.—The healing art of "laying on of hands" was depicted in symbols, inscriptions, and written characters.
- 3000 B.C.—Magic and natural methods using such ingredients as herbs, body parts of animals, and roots were used as healing agents in Egypt. The Egyptians boasted that Imhotep was the god of healing.

- 3000 B.C.—The Greeks also had a god of medicine named Aesculapius, the son of Apollo. The sick spent one or more nights in temples dedicated to Aesculapius. The remedies prescribed were revealed in a dream. The treatment often involved having a big, nonpoisonous yellow snake lick the diseased parts of the patient. Opiates were often given, which could account for reports of dreams and visions. Exorcisms of demons, purgatives, massages, and mineral baths were prescribed as healing agents.

- 2000 B.C.—Acupuncture became a predominant method of treatment in China.

- 2000 B.C.—In the Old Testament, healing was mainly supernatural; it was religious.

- 500 B.C.—Hippocrates, known as the father of modern medicine, described illness in terms of four bodily fluids (blood, phlegm, yellow bile, and bile). He succeeded in moving the practice of healing from purely a religious or magical rite into a medical science. The kiss of serpents was supplemented with dietary rules and regulations. Yet Hippocrates is also credited as saying, "Things are not a varying degree divine or human, but God is in all things." This new school of thought had high moral ideals and a developed code of ethics—evident in the Hippocratic oath, which today is the standard of medical ethics. Hippocrates did not establish a science of medicine; he snatched it from the hands of superstition and made it an art. He also described mental illness as a disease of the brain.

Jesus—The Great Physician

Jesus Christ appeared on the scene as medicine was evolving from sorcery to science. The Jewish environment into which Jesus was born had many sanitary and hygienic practices. However, most believed that disease was a result of demons and that only God could cast out the demons. The technique used for healing was command and the laying on of hands as described in the New Testament.

A great deal of the record of Jesus' life is devoted to his healing ministry. As we move through the Gospels of Matthew, Mark, Luke, and John, we find that the historic accounts of his healing cover all sorts of maladies. Among them were:

- Fever and leprosy
- Blindness
- Palsy (which might be the aftermath of a stroke)
- Dropsy (which a modern physician might diagnose as heart failure or cirrhosis)
- Infirmities in the bones (arthritis)
- Issues of blood (tumors of the uterus or cervix)
- Foaming at the mouth (epilepsy)
- Deafness
- Lameness
- Demon possession (mental illness)
- Attaching a body part (as in the account of the high priest's servant whose ear was cut off with a sword; Jesus placed it back on and the man was healed)

In each case, Jesus used his direct authority to accomplish healing. For centuries the followers and critics of Jesus have tried to understand his healings. They have been called miracles because they seem to have no explanation.

While we cannot fully explain these miracles of Jesus, we do know that he used the healing formula of his day—command and suggestion—backed by his divine authority. Some of his healings consisted of calling out the unclean spirits among those who were demon possessed. A modern medical doctor might explain casting out demons as a psychological method of catharsis that reconnects the different parts of a person's personality that may have been walled off from each other due to trauma at an early age. The sudden and complete healing of the mind, as inferred by Jesus' healing of the lunatic, however, is seldom accomplished by any psychological technique known today.

The three years of Jesus' public ministry were lived in an environment of human suffering and oppression. People might often respond favorably to suggestion. We believe, however, that Jesus' healing ministry was not simply the result of suggestion. We do not rule out the direct and supernatural influence of God (who Jesus is). Because he is God, Jesus could decide to miraculously and sovereignly heal someone.

In many cases, though, Jesus chose to work through the natural laws he had established. Why shouldn't he, since he made them all? If a modern physician could have accompanied Jesus on his rounds of mercy, he probably would have encountered conditions he could identify, such as neurosis, fear, anxiety, insomnia, nervousness, hysteria, and depression. Some of these conditions, so familiar to today's physicians, certainly could have existed during the time of Jesus' healing ministry. Through the technique of direct command, these psychological issues may have been relieved and the patient made well.

The important thing to note is that Jesus possessed divine insight through which he could recognize the cause and institute the cure. He himself said to those whom he had commissioned to minister in his name, "Greater things than these shall you do." Since the time of Jesus, faith healers have performed miracles that seem to confirm these words of Jesus. Could Jesus also have been referring to the "greater things" in healing brought about by Pasteur's work in curing rabies, Lister's work in antiseptic healing, Koch's work in tuberculosis, Jenner's work in smallpox, Morton's work in anesthetics, Banting's work in diabetes, Fleming's work in infections, or Salk's work with polio? On and on it has gone, from illness to cure for many diseases since Jesus' time.

We believe that all healing is divine. However one might try to explain the recorded healings of Jesus, the simple fact remains that the patient's faith was a key factor in the healing process. Surrounding his healings Jesus made statements such as "if you have faith" or "unless you have faith." One woman had an ailment that our doctors today might diagnose as a uterine

tumor or other disease responsible for chronic menstrual bleed-
ing. She approached Jesus from behind and touched the hem
of his garment, and "she said to herself, 'If only I may touch His
garment, I shall be made well.' But Jesus turned around, and
when He saw her He said, 'Be of good cheer, daughter; your faith
has made you well.' And the woman was made well from that
hour" (Matt. 9:21–22). Jesus' divine power caused the healing,
but it appears that her faith also helped make it happen.

Jesus focused on the healing of the whole person: body,
mind, and spirit. He pointed out that the thoughts of a person
are key to achieving health. As recorded in Matthew, "Do you
not yet understand that whatever enters the mouth goes into
the stomach and is eliminated? But those things which proceed
out of the mouth come from the heart, and they defile a man.
For out of the heart proceed evil thoughts, murders, adulteries,
fornications, thefts, false witness, blasphemies. These are the
things which defile a man, but to eat with unwashed hands does
not defile a man" (Matt. 15:17–20). Jesus is not minimizing the
importance of proper nutrition and hygiene. He is saying that
having a good attitude and spirit are essential for good health.

Faith Healing

Early Christians believed that sickness could be healed
through prayer. James, who was the half brother of Jesus,
wrote in his letter to the early church, "Is anyone among you
sick? Let him call for the elders of the church, and let them pray
over him, anointing him with oil in the name of the Lord. And
the prayer of faith will save the sick, and the Lord will raise him
up" (James 5:14–15).

In these early years of the church, caring for the sick was a
unique contribution of Christianity. The pagans did not care
for their sick in any organized fashion, and the Jewish community provided care primarily for its own. The Christian church,
on the other hand, offered care to sick people, Christians and
non-Christians alike. This practice has continued throughout

history with the establishment of medical missions, hospitals, and health centers all over the world.

Throughout the centuries since the healing ministry of Jesus on earth, many Christians have been involved in nontraditional medical healing practices. Many faith-healing ministries have become widely renowned centers of healing. A case in point is the shrine at Lourdes, France. The town of Lourdes is situated high in the Pyrenees on the banks of the mountain stream Gave du Pau.

On February 11, 1858, Bernadette Soubirous, a peasant girl of fourteen who was being prepared for her First Communion, saw a niche above a grotto in an ancient rock, the Massabille, and an apparition of the Virgin Mary. This apparition appeared to the girl nineteen times in all. During one of these visions, she was directed to drink and to wash her face in the corner of the cave. She saw only mud, but she dug with her hands and uncovered a spring at which cures of a miraculous nature were shortly thereafter reported. This spring has since brought thousands of people to Lourdes for healing.

Through the years since 1858 many people who had not responded to any other treatment were reportedly healed. Nearly two million sufferers have visited the shrine since its establishment. Every pilgrim to the site must have a certificate signed by a physician, stating the nature of his or her affliction. At dawn the patient is taken to the grotto, where he or she hears Mass and receives Holy Communion while the priest moves from patient to patient. The patient then steps into a tank filled with water from the spring. The helpless are lowered on webbed slings. All bathe in the same water, which is changed daily.

In the afternoon the sick are gathered around the church, and the procession of the Blessed Sacrament begins. It is at this time that most of the cures occur. When a healing is announced, the subject is moved to the hospital and examined by the medical staff. If a miraculous healing appears to have taken place, the medical committee makes a record of the case. Then the patient must be watched for a year by his or her personal physician and at some point returns to Lourdes for a final checkup. The case is then certified as a "miraculous cure."

These cures at Lourdes have been studied by physicians throughout the world. The case studies indicate that many of these patients were chronically and seriously ill. They were carefully diagnosed and received routine treatments, which were ineffective. What is the explanation for these miraculous healings? The records indicate that the cases were not "fixed" nor were their histories false. Unfortunately, no figures are available on the percentage of patients who were cured or how long their wellness continued. It is difficult to label all of these healings as simply coincidence. As for the patients who have recovered after their pilgrimage to Lourdes, the only thing they know is that they have been cured.

It is senseless to quibble over whether the cure was physical or psychological. It has been claimed that the waters of Lourdes are medicinal. Studies of these waters, however, reveal no unique properties that make them any different from other cold springs in the area. Yet the cures cannot be dismissed as purely imaginary. These patients were made well!

The common element in most of these cases is *extremis* (meaning "at the end of the line"). Most patients had prolonged illnesses and had been under the care of physicians who passed them on to specialists or gave up on them. At that point they reached out to the Divine Physician. Through their faith, as the Bible says, they were healed. That healing needs no explanation. Its source is in God.

In addition to Lourdes and other healing shrines, "faith healers" have reported miraculous cures as a result of faith and prayer. Some of these healings are well documented. Many of them occurred when the patient had tried everything else without success.

All of these Christian healers say that they do not heal; only God heals. They are simply the point of contact or conduit that God uses to heal. These healing events vary in magnitude and intensity. They may occur in homes, nursing care facilities, or hospitals with only one person and the patient present. The person may be a minister or other trained clergy or may be a layperson with the gift of healing. That person may anoint the patient with oil and pray after affirming the healing. Or he or she may not use oil but instead lay hands on the patient, recite a healing litany, and pray. Sometimes the healer may join hands with the family and friends of the patient and pray. Sometimes the patient may be in a coma, and the healing rites are performed without their conscious awareness. The methods used for these healing occasions will usually depend upon the religious tradition of the person presiding.

Since the popularity of televised faith-healing events, some ministers with "special healing gifts" have become familiar to the public. They have held their healing services in churches, halls, auditoriums, big tents, arenas, and stadiums.

We have watched them conduct healing services where miraculous healings appear to be taking place. We have read books giving detailed information and medical data about these healings, verifying the illness and the cure. Since the middle of the twentieth century, several popular faith healers have emerged. Most of these healing services are similar, with inspiring music, dynamic messages, and many people who want to be healed. The procedure goes as follows: The patient, if possible, declares his or her faith to be healed. The healer next places hands on the candidate for healing and prays. The prayer is often given in the terms of command and assert. Such phrases as "in the name of Jesus, stand up and walk!" or "your pain is gone" are often used. The healer may apply a bit of hand pressure on the candidate's forehead or wherever the healing touch is being applied. Frequently the candidate will fall down, as in a swoon, where someone is usually present to assist in the falling. Kathryn Kuhlman, whose book *I Believe in Miracles* was included with my (Chet's) book *Peace and Power through Prayer* in a Guideposts two-in-one book edition, explained to me that the swooning is actually falling in the Spirit. The setting, service environment, group dynamics, need and faith of the candidate for healing, and the healing commands may all contribute to the swooning. But it is not hand pressure or technique on the part of the healer that cause the falling. She also reminded me that the falling frequently happens but is not necessarily the point of healing. God is the point of healing.

Some of these well-known faith healers of the twentieth century are:

- Oral Roberts
- Kathryn Kuhlman
- Benny Hinn
- Kenneth Copeland
- Paul Young-gi Cho of Korea
- Kenneth Hagen
- Many seen on TBN (the Christian TV network)

Through their ministries and the ministries of thousands of others, people have reported healing during such group services. In fact, Daniel Johnson and other researchers at Virginia Commonwealth University surveyed a random sampling of 586 persons in Richmond, Virginia, to determine how often physical cures result from faith healing. The question asked was, "Have you ever experienced a healing of a serious disease or physical condition that you believed resulted from prayer or considered to be a divine healing?" Of the 586 persons surveyed, 84 responded that they had (14.3 percent). Divine healing, in this study, was not a rare phenomenon. [1]

Faith healing, divine healing, and *miracle healing* are all terms used to describe healing that occurs outside the normal accepted medical route. Everyone who has been healed through these methods rejoices that healing has occurred. But we should not categorize healing as either strictly due to medicine or strictly due to faith. All healing is divine, all healing requires faith, and all healing is miraculous in that people are made whole again.

Prayer and Healing

Whatever the healing method, prayer is often a major contributing factor. Some have said that prayer may be a factor in assisting the doctor in healing the body. Others would say that it is the other way around; that the doctor may be a factor in assisting the prayers of a devout person. The bottom line is that the same body is healed. We see this synergism in healing all the time.

In September 1984 I (Chet) was in Colorado Springs, Colorado, doing some location filming for my television show *Facing Life*. Our producer, Bill Welsh, the popular sports and news commentator and the voice of the Pasadena Rose Parade for many years, and I were planning to fly to Colorado to start filming on Monday. My son Stephen, who was involved in television production in Colorado Springs, was working on this filming session. He telephoned me the week before saying that he was not feeling well and that his doctor thought he might have an ulcer. I traveled to Colorado from California the weekend before the filming. Steve came to the filming but was not feeling well enough to give his full attention. During the lunch break, we went by his office and found that he had a phone message from his doctor, asking him to come to his office immediately. On the Friday before, the radiologist had taken X rays to determine the location of the problem. The X ray had indicated something wrong in Steve's chest area. The doctor told us that it could be tuberculosis or a possibly cancerous tumor. He ordered Steve into the hospital immediately for testing and observation. That night, an oncologist examined him and discovered a problem in his testicles (Steve had served in Vietnam jungles and had been exposed to Agent Orange). Following a full-body scan, testicular cancer was discovered. Surgery was scheduled for early the following morning. The surgeon indicated that the cancer had spread through much of Steve's body. Because the cancer had metastasized, the oncologist ordered chemotherapy to begin immediately following the surgery. He said Steve had a 50 percent chance of survival. He said he would do his best to help bring him through, and also that he believed in the power of prayer. We agreed to pray.

Steve endured six months of chemotherapy. He lost weight, lost his hair, and was very sick during this time. Throughout the drug therapy and physical therapy, he had a positive mental attitude toward his own healing, and the prayer and support of family and friends. Afterward, he was completely healed of his cancer. Prayer may be the synergistic agent that brings it all together and makes healing happen.

Integration of Faith and Medicine

Many clinics, foundations, and medical centers in the United States and around the world now include a focus on the mind and spirit, as well as on the physical body. For example, Duke University has a new Center for Integrative Medicine that includes the best of traditional medicine with alternative therapies, psychological and social therapies, and spirituality. Unless explicitly Christian, most of these integrative medicine centers or clinics like the one at Duke usually employ an Eastern form of spirituality (mindfulness meditation) that may be foreign to many Americans. Many hospitals across the country, however, retain a religious affiliation and include praying by chaplains or pastoral counselors as an option to pursue in addition to traditional medicine.

Over the centuries, discussion has continued about whether faith has negative, neutral, or positive effect on health. For centuries religion regulated and controlled medical care. In the Middle Ages, the church was the official body that issued medical licenses to physicians. Many physicians were monks or priests. The nursing profession emerged from religious orders devoted to caring for the sick. Religious groups were also responsible for building and staffing the first hospitals.

Over the past five hundred years, the church began to share this responsibility with the state and the secular scientific establishment. Eventually it lost its influence over the medical profession. In the past fifty years, there has been an active rapprochement between these healing traditions of faith and medicine.

2

STRESS CAN KILL YOU

We face many things every day that cause us to feel stressed. To stress means to put under strain. We are learning that these mental and physical tensions cause us great damage. Research has shown that as these tensions accumulate, a person becomes more susceptible to physical illness, mental and emotional distress, and accidental injuries. Various parts of the body are directly affected by stress: brain, skin, hair, mouth, lungs, heart, digestive tract, reproductive organs, bladder, and muscles.

Stress may be caused by environment, personality, mental attitudes, or events occurring around us. Some of these factors are beyond our control. We can, however, control how we react to the stressors in our lives. We ought to recognize that we are overloading our ability to handle stress, but we keep piling it on or allowing others to pile it on. One reason for this is *denial*. We simply do not believe anything bad could happen to us.

Some stressful activities may have a higher priority for us than our health. We may be driven by fun, pleasure, money, power, glamour, or social acceptance. These priorities may create great stress. We may deliberately decide not to clean up our act until later in life. Our attitude may be "let's make hay while the sun shines" or "let's eat, drink, and be merry." It is certainly true that at various seasons of our lives we are motivated by different drives. However, during each season we should focus on our health and wholeness.

Hal was a perfectionist. Outwardly he appeared to be at the peak of success. Hal was a sales professional and worked day and night to be the salesman of the month, every month, in his organization. He became depressed if he didn't get that honor each month. Hal was punctual for all his sales meetings and appointments. He was irritated if other people were not right on time.

At home Hal was a tyrant. Everything had to be perfect. His lawn was without weeds and always the best in the neighborhood. The furniture looked as though it had never been used. Hilda, his wife, was an excellent cook. Hal loved to eat and demanded big dinners served at certain times each day. The plates and silverware had to be placed just right. Hal ravished his food. When dinner was over, Hal lit a cigarette (he was a chain smoker) and headed for the den. This was his hobby room, but it was really a *trophy* room, containing a collection of guns, knives, armor, and gadgets of all shapes, sizes, and descriptions. His collection was overwhelming. Everything was in its place, and nothing could be touched or moved. This was Hal's stuff, his own private museum.

Hal and Hilda had no children. They took great pride in inviting newcomers to the community for one of Hilda's delicious dinners. Following dinner their visitors were shown Hal's amazing collection, and all looked forward to a return visit. However, by the second visit they felt smothered by Hal's ego and dominance and bored by his self-preoccupation. They chose not to return again. Hal became angry over their "lack of appreciation."

Hal and Hilda attended church where Hal sang in the choir. He was a fair singer but wanted to be the best. Yet if the choir needed to work on a portion of the anthem because one part or a singer had not sung it right, Hal became furious and commented on his busy schedule. In time, the choirmaster talked to Hal about his inappropriate outbursts, so Hal quit the choir. Eventually Hal was all tied up within himself. From this self-pressure came great stress.

At forty-three, Hal began having chest pains and breathing problems. He was overweight and exercised very little. He worked constantly, even when he was trying to relax. The doctor told Hal he had symptoms of a heart problem. Hal refused to listen; he was in denial. He thought he could control anything, even this "little heart problem." Three months later when Hal was lifting a heavy piece of highly prized war apparatus, he had a severe coronary occlusion. The paramedics arrived in minutes after Hilda's frantic call. Hal died en route to the hospital. His doctor said that stress killed him. Sadly, Hal didn't clean up his stress act in time.

Stress Management

A variety of stress management techniques might have prolonged Hal's life, such as:

- Maintaining good social relationships
- Eliminating negative and irrational thinking
- Practicing positive thinking
- Organizing life better
- Discontinuing a smoking habit
- Taking it easy on alcohol and caffeine
- Getting plenty of rest
- Developing a hobby that's fun and not demanding
- Exercising regularly
- Practicing relaxation techniques
- Developing a prayer life

Studies have shown that psychological stress of even brief duration can cause remarkable changes in the body. Alan Breier and his colleagues at the Maryland Psychiatric Research Center of the University of Maryland School of Medicine in Baltimore demonstrated that lack of control over even mildly unpleasant stimuli in ten healthy human volunteers produced elevated hormone levels, greater sympathetic nervous system activity, and higher electrodermal activity.[1] Similarly, in a study of twenty-two older women, John Cacioppo and others from the Department of Psychology and the Brain, Behavior, Immunity, Health Program at Ohio State University found that brief psychological stress caused increased heart rate, elevated adrenaline levels, and diminished immune responses.[2]

Interpersonal relationships, in particular, may give rise to stress that affects nervous system activity, hormones, and immune function. Studying ninety newlywed couples, Janice Kiecolt-Glaser and other researchers at Ohio State University found that those who displayed more negative or hostile behaviors during a thirty-minute discussion of marital problems showed greater decreases in natural killer cell activity (a "natural killer cell" is an immune cell in the blood that kills viruses, bacteria, and cancer cells) and other immune functions and more sustained increases in blood pressure.[3]

Pastors spend a great deal of time as personal counselors with couples having serious difficulties in their relationships. Sometimes the stress is due to one person having an affair. This often heightens the hostility and adds to the stress factor in the marriage. Sometimes the problem is finances or trouble with the children. Or perhaps someone in the family is sick or dying. I (Chet) discovered as a pastor that if I could get the couple to begin talking about their situation and expressing their feelings openly and honestly, we could begin to break down the hostility and relieve the stress that each spouse experienced. Since they had selected me, a minister, for counsel, the couple was not surprised when I suggested that we pray before the session ended. Many times I would ask each of them to pray out loud. When they cooperated in doing this, we were often well on our way toward a healthy resolution. Prayer added the healing power of God to their situation, and I found that it also humbled and quieted their hostility.

Infection and Stress

Feelings of sadness, depression, and exhaustion resulting from chronic stress can cause a variety of neuroendocrine changes, including elevations of blood hormones and adrenaline. Numerous studies have found impaired lymphocyte function, including weaker natural killer cell activity, in persons with depression. Roger Bartrop's research team from the University of New South Wales in Sydney, Australia, was the first to report weaker immune cell function in grieving persons who had recently lost a spouse.[4] By the sixth week after the death of a loved one, immune cells were not working as well in grieving subjects compared to controls. More recently, in a two-year study of sixty-six patients with terminal infections, Jane Leserman and her colleagues at the University of North Carolina, Chapel Hill, found stress and depression predicted decreases in several measures of immune function and in the patients' ability to fight off the infections.[5]

A number of studies suggest that stress-induced immune changes are large enough to worsen health outcomes. For example, stress may cause greater susceptibility to viral, bacterial, and fungal infections. Kiecolt-Glaser's group found that stressed caregivers of people with Alzheimer's disease were significantly more likely than control subjects to experience depression, which in turn was associated with weaker immune function and an increased risk of infection, especially colds, flu, and pneumonia.[6]

I (Chet) knew a young mother with two small children, one in her "terrible twos" and the other in his "feisty fours." No wonder this mother was under stress. She also had living with her an aging grandmother with serious memory problems caused by dementia. The stress created by the demands from these three dependents caused this young mother to become depressed. She experienced chronic fatigue and had a constant cold. Allergy tests and other examinations could find no treatable medical problem. When her grandmother moved to a skilled nursing facility, the mother could focus on her children, who soon became more manageable. Furthermore, her constant cold symptoms gradually went away.

Stress may impair immune responses to viral infections in the young and healthy, as well as in the old and sick. Vaccinating forty-eight second-year medical students on the last day of a three-day examination series, Kiecolt-Glaser's group found that academic stress decreased these students' ability to respond immunologically to the hepatitis B vaccine.[7] This finding indicated that their immune systems weren't working right. Students who developed an immune response were significantly less stressed and anxious than students who failed to do so.

Studying stress-induced susceptibility to viral infection more directly, Sheldon Cohen and other researchers at Carnegie Mellon University infected 394 healthy volunteers ages 20 to 55 with a cold virus. They then measured levels of stress to see whether people who were more stressed out were more likely to get sick with the cold. Both respiratory infections and colds increased in almost direct proportion to increases in psychological stress.[8]

Stress may also influence recovery from infection. Dwight Evans and his colleagues at the University of North Carolina, Chapel Hill, examined the relationship between stressful life events and disease worsening in ninety-three patients with terminal infections, assessing subjects and controls over a forty-two-month period.[9] HIV-positive men with high life stress experienced much more rapid worsening of their disease than those with low life stress. The risk of disease progression doubled for each stressful life event the subjects experienced.

You have probably seen the great Hall of Famer, Magic Johnson, interviewed on television. In the midst of enormous success as a leading professional basketball star, he was informed that he tested positive for HIV. He gave up his basketball career and prepared himself for the battle to fight this dreaded disease. He now appears very well, is a national spokesperson for AIDS, and has become a very successful businessman. Whenever he is interviewed on the subject of his health, he gives great credit to what he calls "mind and medicine over matter." He talks openly about the power of a positive mental attitude and faith in his recovery. Magic Johnson and his family attend and support their church in Los Angeles, California.

Cancer and Stress

There is some indication that psychological distress may increase your likelihood of getting cancer even if you're healthy. However, evidence is especially strong to support the role of immune factors in affecting the course of cancer once it has already started to grow and spread. In a study of seventy-five women with breast cancer, who were carefully examined for three months, Sandra Levy and her colleagues at the Pittsburgh Cancer Institute, University of Pittsburgh, found, both at the start of the study and three months later, that those who felt depressed and tired all the time didn't possess as strong natural killer cells.[10] In another study, Levy's group examined mood and time to death following the return of breast cancer in thirty-six women who had experienced breast cancer in the past.[11] Positive affect (joy) predicted longer survival after cancer recurrence even after taking into account how long physicians thought patients would live and how widely spread their tumors were. Similar findings were reported by Roberts and other investigators at Ohio State University who examined how quickly women diagnosed with uterine or cervical cancer got worse.[12] In that study, women who were depressed had significantly more lymph nodes positive for cancer when they were examined at a later date.

In 1984, I (Chet) was a new member of the staff at the Crystal Cathedral in Garden Grove, California. Another new staff member, Greg Anderson, had recently had a lung removed. Four months after the surgery, he shared with the staff that his medical team told him the cancer had metastasized throughout his lymph system and he had just thirty days to live. Despite this prognosis, a combination of chemotherapy, his healthy mental attitude, and prayer enabled Greg to beat the cancer. Today, he is the author of many books on the subject of wellness, including his international best-seller *The Cancer Conqueror,* which has been translated into eighteen languages. The founding chairman and CEO of the Cancer Recovery Foundation of America, Greg is considered one of the leading spokespersons for the integration of the mental, spiritual, and traditional medical aspects of healing.

In his writings, eloquent public speaking, and work with over fifteen thousand cancer survivors, Greg has consistently argued that "the body's healing capacity is directly linked to one's mental and spiritual well-being. Embracing healthy beliefs and attitudes, learning to effectively resolve emotional distress, and moving in the direction of greater joy and gratitude all have a direct impact on our physical health."[13]

Greg Anderson's own experience, and that of thousands with whom he has worked, testifies to this truth: Stress and the relief of stress might affect the course of cancer.

Stress and Wound Healing

Some of the most exciting research in this area examines psychological stress as a predictor of the speed of wound healing. Most people don't realize that when they get a cut, are involved in an accident, or undergo surgery, being under a lot of stress can actually slow down the healing of their wounds. Scientists have discovered that the process of wound healing depends on having a healthy immune system. For example, Kiecolt-Glaser's group at Ohio State University studied thirteen older persons caring for family members who had Alzheimer's disease.[14] Their goal was to determine if the stress of caregiving impaired wound healing in these subjects. Wounds in stressed caregivers took significantly longer (24 percent) to heal compared to nonstressed controls. Interestingly, the same result was found when the experiment was repeated in eleven young dental students.[15] The first wound was made during summer vacation and the second wound was made three days before the first major examination of the term. Students took an average of three days longer (40 percent) to heal the wounds during the stressful examination period, compared to wounds made during the more relaxing summer.

Stress and the Entire Person

Years ago a wise doctor said, "Illness is not simply a matter of what you are eating but also what's eating you." A clear link exists between stress and illness.

In a section on the effects of stress on the physical body, the *American Medical Association Family Medical Guide* confirms what we've been relating here: Research has shown that as stresses accumulate an individual becomes increasingly susceptible to physical illness, mental and emotional problems, and accidental injuries as well.

Certain parts of the body seem to be particularly susceptible to stress-related disease. For example:

- *The brain.* Many scientists agree that stress in the form of depression, fear, or anxiety may lead to changes in the brain that could increase the risk of developing Alzheimer's disease or other conditions such as a stroke and possibly Parkinson's disease.
- *The mouth.* Have you ever noticed that a cold sore might develop when you are going through a stressful time? Physicians and dentists say that mouth ulcers and other oral problems may have their origin in stress.
- *The lungs.* We have all observed that the condition of people with asthma or emphysema worsens when they are subjected to high levels of mental or emotional stress.
- *The heart.* Attacks of angina and disturbances of heart rate and rhythm often occur at the same time as or shortly after a period of stress. I (Chet) experienced angina pains and shortness of breath at particular stressful times in my life, eventually resulting in emergency open-heart surgery. Of

course, high cholesterol, lack of regular exercise, improper
diet, and inadequate rest were factors in creating the problem—but stress may have brought it to the "heart attack"
stage.

- *The digestive tract.* Gastritis, stomach and duodenal ulcers,
  ulcerative colitis, and irritable colon may all be caused or
  aggravated by stress.

- *The reproductive organs.* Many specialists in the field now
  agree that menstrual disorders and male impotence may
  be the result of stress-related problems.

- *The skin.* Have you ever had skin problems, or know someone who has, such as eczema and psoriasis when under
  great stress?

Stress is often related to change, and changes are an integral
part of life. We are constantly called upon to make adjustments
to a new environment, a new person, or a new challenge. We
cannot escape change. Many significant or critical turning points
in our lives develop stress. Some of these changes have a greater
influence than the others upon our stress levels. We should
evaluate our stress burdens. As you look at changes in your
own life, you may see patterns of events that often generate
great stress. Many doctors and medical societies have rankings
and measurements of events that cause great stress. Regardless
of the point system used, there seems to be general agreement
that certain events and changes create more stress than others.
In descending order, the following events may be measured as
heavy stress factors:

- Your spouse has died.
- Your child has died.
- You have been separated from your life's partner.
- You have been told you have a serious illness.
- A close relative has died.
- You are or recently were hospitalized.
- You have recently married.

- You have reconciled with your spouse.
- You have become a parent.
- Your children are having problems.
- You will soon become a parent.
- You have lost your job.
- You are about to retire.
- You have recently retired.
- You have had a brush with the law.
- A close friend has died.
- You are in a lawsuit.
- Your finances are in trouble.
- You are experiencing sexual problems.
- You are having "in-law" problems.
- You are moving into a new location.
- You are worried about your financial future.
- A family member is bugging you.
- You are having trouble with a friend.
- You are having trouble with a coworker.
- You are having trouble with a neighbor.
- You are remodeling your house.
- You are changing your business structure.
- You are burdened with debt.

These are a few of the major changes that occur in many of our lives. Look at this list and evaluate the load you are carrying because of change.

A great deal of medical research seems to suggest our stressful events, and our body's physiological reaction to these events, can increase the risk of disease. For example, it is rather common for people to report chest pains, breathing problems, or dizziness during high-peak loads of emotional distress. Heart attacks may be associated with these high stress levels.

In addition to life events, personality characteristics may provoke stress. We have all heard about type A and type B personalities. Type A's, for example, seem to be hurried, competitive, and highly desirous to be productive and to achieve. We often call this kind of person a workaholic. Type B's are usually less in a hurry, more easily satisfied with their status, and easier to be around. Now, while these labels do not fully describe a person, they may be helpful in interpreting some illnesses. Researchers have suggested, after many studies, that type A's may have up to twice the risk of coronary artery disease as type B's. Personality traits seem to be related to stress. We may not be able to change our personality traits, but we may be able to manage our personality more effectively.

A series of stressful life events or your own personality traits may not predict that you are a candidate for a heart attack or other serious illness. However, you may be able to raise or lower your risks by your own behavior and attitude. The first thing to do is to recognize the symptoms of stress and to modify your behavior and attitude.

Remember, stress can kill you.

3

Prayer Can Help Heal You

There now seems to be little question that the body is affected by stress and negative thoughts. Sir William Osler, the brilliant Canadian physician, suggested that the outcome of tuberculosis had more to do with what went on in the patient's mind than what went on in his lungs! Osler seems to be repeating what Hippocrates, the founder of modern medicine, observed much earlier—that he would rather know what sort of person has a disease than what disease a person has. This seems to confirm what the writer of Proverbs penned centuries ago: "For as he thinks within himself, so he is" (Prov. 23:7 NASB).

Since medical research has documented the effect of our minds and emotions on our state of health, it would seem that a chief concern of ours should be to alter our thoughts and emotions from negative to positive. How do we do that?

Many techniques have been tried, including visualization, hypnosis, guided imagery, transcendental meditation, biofeedback, group therapy, stress-relieving drugs, yoga, and psychological counseling. Each of these techniques may have value. However, there exists a potentially greater stress-reducing activity: prayer. If prayer can help to relieve stress, as much research is now beginning to show, then we may have a scientific explanation for how prayer works in healing people. We are not discounting that prayer most undoubtedly works through supernatural means as well. However, it does appear that our brains and bodies are wired in such a way that praying to God and having faith in God's love and power can make a real difference in our health in ways even scientists can understand.

Science and Prayer

Unfortunately, science and prayer have not always seemed compatible. Twenty-three centuries ago, however, Plato pointed out that it was an error for the physicians of his day to separate the spirit from the body.

We believe that separating the spirit from the body has retarded the healing process of the whole person. In modern times, many medical students emerge from their studies with their sights trained on the laboratory rather than on the examination room. They have been trained as pure scientists rather than as whole-person doctors. As a result, the gulf between doctor and patient has widened. Prayer and positive mental attitudes are often not included in the medical bag. Many physicians consider religion nonessential or even a liability. This scientific exclusiveness may have arisen out of the concept of dualism advocated by the French philosopher René Descartes. The blame for the fragmentation of the human person, however, cannot be placed on scientists alone. Religious leaders have become defensive, and the pulpit sometimes becomes a place for condemning science and its accomplishments.

Today, however, this dualism is changing. Many scientists and theologians are realizing that healing is synergistic. *Synergism* comes from the two Greek words *syn* (meaning "together") and *ergon* (meaning "work"). That is what medicine and prayer must do; they must work together. *Webster's New World Dictionary* defines *synergism* as "the simultaneous action of separate agencies which, together, have greater total effect than the sum of their individual effects."

We see synergism at work around us constantly. For example:

In theater. On a particular night the show is fantastic. The actors are the same as every other performance. The script and set design are the same. The theater is filled with people as it is every night. Yet as the curtain is lowered on the final act, the audience breaks forth in applause like no other night. The next day the theater critics are calling it a "magical" performance. What happened? Synergism. The combination of the cast and audience at that particular performance came together in an extraordinary way.

In sports. In a particular season the team that had lost most of its games the previous season is now winning all its games. Most of the players are the same as the year before. The coaches are the same. They played the same schedule. Their home stadium remained the same. The spectators are the same. Something happened to give the team a winning season. What? Synergism. Everything worked together to make it happen.

In medicine. A group of drugs are combined by chemists into a compound drug. The combination of the individual drugs is found to have much greater healing effect than each of the drugs administered separately. This is synergism.

In the human body. There are over six hundred named muscles. Each muscle is made up of bundles of closely interlocking muscle fibers, which vary in length and design. Some of the muscle fibers contract and relax very quickly while others are designed for long-term contraction. It is the working together of the entire muscular system that gives us posture and movement. This is synergism.

In healing. We believe that the working together of medicine, physicians, science, patient, and God is what produces healing. The word *healing* comes from an Anglo-Saxon word meaning "to make whole" and carries with it the idea of restoration to a normal condition. Immediately we are aware of the close association of health and healing. Healing involves restoring to a condition of wholeness; health is that condition of being whole. The healing process is often time-consuming and complex. Whether the healing of a wound in the flesh or of a distraught and anxious mind, a diseased organ or a fearful and anxious spirit, the process is essentially the same—the restoration of that which is broken or fractured back to that which is whole and complete.

The art and science of physical healing in modern times has become the responsibility of the medical doctor and other trained professionals in the health-care system. They have been taught to recognize the causes for physical problems and to find ways to assist nature in the recovery process. Through the use of medicine, the doctor has been able to give nature a boost in manufacturing antibodies to combat invading germs. Through the use of surgery, the doctor has been able to remove the tissue or organ that is causing malfunction. Through the use of certain devices and physical therapy, the doctor is able to aid in the restorative process. Each of these methods of healing has benefited millions of people needing help.

Alongside these long-established and recognized healing agents is prayer. Many physicians will say that they had been unable to cure a patient because his or her body seemed to refuse to cooperate. A mental depression, severe anxiety, or rigidity caused by guilt or malice seems to have closed off the natural healing routes. This is where prayer comes into the picture.

Dr. Paul Dudley White, an eminent heart specialist, stated that his experience with patients had convinced him that prayer in many instances had a powerful influence in healing. Many physicians have made it a regular practice to pray at the bedside of a patient or at the operating table. They do not think that prayer is a substitute for medicines, surgery, diet, rest, or any other established medical procedures. They recognize prayer as a powerful force alongside these other healing agents.

If prayer has the potential to produce healing along with drugs, surgery, and other therapies, then prayer should be ranked right up there with all the great abilities humankind has unleashed for healing of the human body. Prayer heals because it links us with God, who created us. We believe that all healing is "divine healing," whether natural or supernatural.

Does God also heal people from physical health problems outside the use of medicine? Yes, we believe he does. Too many people have experienced divine healing to conclude otherwise. If God does heal, how does he do this? One possibility is that he sovereignly and mysteriously alters the course of nature: In that case, God acts contrary to nature in order to heal our bodies, which otherwise would be destined for disability or death due to illness. This is what we call a miracle. Doctors cannot easily explain such cases and are sometimes amazed, since there is no scientific explanation. The patient takes a course completely against what medical knowledge would predict. We who are healed in this miraculous way are eternally grateful for having been given a second chance at life. It is like the man in the Bible who was born blind, but could suddenly see after Jesus touched his eyes. No medical explanation is possible. God breaks through the established order of nature and creation.

A second way that God might heal is in a way that doctors and scientists cannot identify or prove as a miracle, and yet the course of nature is still altered. In this instance, nature is changed in a subtle way, perhaps at the atomic or subatomic level. With the emergence of quantum physics, we know that alterations in nature may occur in barely perceptible ways at the quantum level that may alter the course of events. Furthermore, bear in mind that God exists outside of time and can make alterations in nature in such a way that he could heal someone and then alter the entire course of history so that doctors and scientists could not detect anything out of the ordinary. This explanation is important to consider because sometimes God can heal people and yet doctors and scientists, using their natural tools of science limited by space and time, may never be able to prove that a healing has occurred.

A third way God might heal people is through our faith and belief in him. Belief activates the natural physiological processes in the body (the immune system, the hormonal system, the circulatory system) to speed healing and recovery. While a lot has been spoken about God's power to heal through miraculous, mysterious, and unexplained ways, much less has been said about how God in some instances may use the very bodies that he created to cause a more rapid healing through scientifically comprehensible processes.

Researchers are learning more and more about how the various parts of the brain are connected to the physiological processes in the body, thereby substantiating such a possibility. This in many respects is itself miraculous. How marvelous it is that our bodies have been created in this way. Indeed the body contains many direct connections between the brain (the center of our will and faith) and the body's natural healing systems.

The brain is unconsciously and continuously communicating back and forth with the immune system, the cardiovascular system, and all major organ systems in the body by releasing hormones and other chemicals from nerve cells. An intricate system of nerves extends from the brain down the spinal cord and then out directly into the lymph nodes, the spleen, the bone marrow, and other primary organs that make up and maintain the immune system.

The brain is also communicating with immune cells in the blood through hormones and other blood proteins known as cytokines. The immune cells, in turn, send chemical messengers back to the brain to complete an intricate feedback loop. The brain also sends signals to the spinal cord telling it to slow down or speed up transmission of pain impulses. Thus, there is every indication that the anatomical pathways exist for the brain to directly impact the experience of pain and the speed of recovery from infections and other diseases, including the healing of wounds following a surgical operation or an accident.

These connections with the brain must exist for some reason. The reason may be to connect our psychological, social, and spiritual lives with our physical bodies so that these can all work together in the healing process. Remember that Jesus did not make much distinction between the mind, the body, and the spirit, but viewed and healed people as whole entities.

We have seen that how we think and feel may significantly impact immune functioning, heart rate, blood pressure, and speed of recovery from disease. In addition, a number of studies are also beginning to show that religious or spiritual activities such as attending church services, reading Scripture, praying, and other forms of religious expression influence a person's well-being and physical health.

For example, a recent study at Duke University demonstrated that a cytokine called interleukin–6 (IL–6) in blood was significantly lower among persons who attended church more often.[1] High IL–6 levels may indicate a weakened immune system, as might be seen in patients with diseases that attack this system. Another study at the University of Iowa also found that lower IL–6 levels were related to spiritual coping among older adults who were under the stress of being forcibly relocated to a different living situation.[2]

Similarly, a study of patients living with chronic terminal infections, conducted by researchers at the University of Miami, found that those who were actively involved in attending religious services, Scripture reading, prayer, or meditation had higher numbers of the key immune system cell designed to fight off the infection. Likewise, a study of over one hundred women with metastatic breast cancer, conducted at Stanford University, found that high levels of religious expression were significantly correlated with higher numbers of natural killer cells, lymphocytes, and other parts of the immune system helpful in destroying cancer cells.[3]

Finally, a series of new studies is now being designed at Johns Hopkins University to observe the effects of group and individual prayer on immune functioning in patients with breast cancer and in patients with congestive heart failure. One of the studies has recently been funded by the National Institutes of Health and represents the first NIH-funded prayer study of this type. In that project, eighty African-American women with early breast cancer are being randomly assigned to either an intensive in-person group prayer intervention or to a control group without prayer. These women will be studied for six months to assess their immune functioning, speed of cancer recurrence, and ultimately, their length of survival.

Thus, we're just beginning to see how devout religious beliefs and practices like prayer may impact our physical bodies through known scientific mechanisms. Again, whether God decides to heal our bodies miraculously and unexplainably, or through the physiological pathways that he designed when he created our bodies, it is still divine healing, wonderful and marvelous, particularly if you are the one healed. And in the end, it really doesn't matter exactly how God heals us, but rather that he loves us and wants us to be whole in body, mind, and spirit.

You may be reading this book and have a physical or emotional problem. You've tried every medical procedure and curative drug that you and your doctor know about, but you are still not well. What can you do? To begin with, don't give up. Have faith that God can heal you. Become involved in your own wellness program. Take more responsibility for your own health, maintaining it through diet, exercise, and careful living, as well as changing your thinking and believing so that this may create in your body the right environment for physical and emotional healing. In addition to all that, add the amazing healing power of God. You lock into that power through prayer. By praying to God and surrendering to him, you allow God to activate the spiritual and physiological mechanisms that lead to wholeness and restoration.

Medicine, surgery, and all the other healing methods that doctors bring into the process are important. However, you have a responsibility and an opportunity to participate in your own healing through prayer.

This gives rise to some tough questions. When we pray, is it the person praying who is doing the healing or is it God who is doing it? Can people heal themselves without God? Can scientists exclude God from the healing process? We believe that healing involves a combination of both what God does and what humans do. Some healing seems to occur without divine intervention. Some healing seems to occur without human intervention.

Most of the time both are necessary. A collaborative relationship between a person and God is necessary, and prayer is the key to that collaboration.

We return now to the story recorded in the ninth chapter of the Gospel of John about a man who had been blind from birth. He was brought to Jesus for healing. Jesus spat on the ground and made clay with the saliva and dirt. Then Jesus placed the clay on the blind man's eyes, instructing him to wash his eyes in the nearby pool of Siloam. The man went and washed the clay off his eyes and immediately could see.

This seemed like a miracle to the crowd who had gathered. Trying to explain what happened, his neighbors said, "Is not this the same man who was blind and sat begging for gifts?" Some said, "Yes, that's the same man." Others said, "He is like him but it may not be the same man." The healed man said, "Yes, I'm that same man." They all began to question him as to what happened. He told them about a man named Jesus who made clay out of dirt, put it on his eyes, and told him to go wash his face, and with that, his eyesight was restored.

Then the religious people got into the act. They brought in the man for further questioning. He repeated the same story about the clay and the healing. The skeptics would not believe him; they thought he was faking. They said, "It is not the same beggar who was blind in our midst." So they called in his parents. However, his parents testified that the man before them was indeed their son who had been blind since birth. They said, "We cannot explain his healing." Then the parents told their inquisitors that their son was old enough to speak for himself.

Still thinking that the healing was a fake, the interrogators asked the healed blind man for a report on Jesus, the healer. In effect they were saying that Jesus was a charlatan and wanted to know what the healed blind man thought about him. Though he could not explain the healing, the man replied, "One thing I know: that though I was blind, now I see" (John 9:25).

This story is a good description of how healing works. Was it the miraculous power of Jesus? Was it the healing powers in the clay or water? Was it the faith of the blind man asking Jesus to restore his sight? It may have been all of these. The important point is that the blind man's sight was restored.

Prayer was the key to his healing. In the Book of James, the writer summed up the importance of prayer for healing when he wrote, "And the prayer of faith will save the sick, and the Lord will raise him up" (James 5:15).

We believe that prayer is one of the greatest sources of healing for the body, the mind, and the spirit. Prayer is powerful—we call it "prayer power." Try it! Practice it! Prayer has great potential to heal and make us whole, so let's use it!

4

WHAT IS PRAYER?

*I*n the last chapter we noted that prayer helps us achieve health and wholeness—physically, mentally, and spiritually. In our culture today, there are many kinds of "prayer." What kind of prayer are *we* discussing? First, let's see what this kind of prayer is not.

Prayer is not mental telepathy or autosuggestion. It is not magic, psychic energy, or human intentionality. Prayer is not merely thinking good thoughts. It is not repeating nonsense syllables, doing breathing exercises, or practicing visualization. None of these terms describe prayer as we use it in this book.

Webster defines *prayer* as "an earnest request to God . . . an utterance of peace to God." Prayer is different from meditation. Webster defines *meditation* as "deep reflection, especially on sacred matters." To meditate means to ponder and think deeply and continuously. Meditation is often self-centered. Prayer is God-centered. Prayer originates in a relationship with God. The more we pray, the deeper that relationship grows.

Prayer is a natural human urge. We have a praying instinct. Prayer, in some form, is as natural to the spirit as eating or sleeping is to the physical body. When we set out to discover what prayer is, we must realize that we are dealing with a natural function of life. Prayer is an innate human experience.

The practice of praying has been found in one form or another in nearly all cultures and among all peoples. Historians have discovered in the records of ancient civilizations the desire and impulse to pray. Prayer is so deeply rooted within us that the reason we pray is that we simply cannot help it. When faced with a sudden crisis, we cry out intuitively: "Oh my God!" Deep in every person lies the desire to pray. It is not an alien practice you must learn, but a natural urge you can cultivate. Since prayer is natural and necessary and has such a profound influence upon the total person—body, mind, and spirit—it is vital that we understand prayer in order to practice it more efficiently.

What, then, is prayer? Prayer is a conversation with God. Prayer is not a monologue. Prayer is dialogue. It is a person-to-person experience. Prayer is essentially a visit with God. It includes speaking, listening, and evaluating. Prayer is probably the loftiest experience within our reach—the ability to connect with the creator and ruler of the universe on a personal level.

Prayer Is Conversation

Webster defines *conversation* as "two or more persons talking together." We may experience this with God. It grows out of a relationship between a person and God. In order to understand this relationship we must first understand the participants. Who's doing the talking? Who's listening? Both the human and the divine are involved in the activity of prayer.

Who Are We?

First, let us look at humans. Who is this creature that stares back when we look in the mirror? The great sages of history have all expressed a fundamental desire to know themselves. The answer to this question makes prayer more meaningful.

As we study humanity, we immediately become aware that we are indeed complex creatures. We see ourselves as physical bodies, intelligent minds, and spiritual beings. The total person—body, mind, and spirit—is involved in the praying experience. In order to understand humans, we must understand our components as well as our totality. Science is one guide that helps us understand what it means to be human.

For example, the science of anatomy explains the parts of the human body—bones, blood vessels, ligaments, skin, glands, organs, and other physical components. The microscope reveals the order and arrangement of the tiny units of which our bodies are composed and which we call cells. Anatomy describes the form of the body, not its activities.

The activity of this structure is explained by the science of physiology. It tells us how movement is caused by the contraction of muscle fibers in obedience to nerve impulses. It describes how sensations travel from the brain, explains the functions of the various organs, and describes the workings of the digestive and the cardiovascular systems.

These sciences of anatomy and physiology help guide us in our understanding of the physical person. Through them we come to understand our structure and function, but it is only the beginning of understanding who and what we are.

How are we related to the rest of life about us? To answer this question we turn to the science of biology. It attempts to explain the origin and activity of all living things, including man. Therefore, in order to understand humans, it is necessary to study ourselves in relation to other living organisms.

But what about the parts of the world that do not seem to be alive? We are directly related to this material realm in which we must live and operate. We turn to the science of physics, which analyzes and describes the properties of matter and formulates physical laws describing the relations of different bodies to one another. We are directly conditioned by and must usually perform in conjunction with these laws.

Now, if we can understand these different areas of science, we have a fair idea of what makes up the animal called "human." But then the question arises: "Where did we come from?" Anthropologists take up the search. They study and interpret the external factors that have been important in the origin and development of our physical and behavioral characteristics as a species. Along comes the sociologist concerned with the relationships between humans. Why do we act as we do with each other? What is our relationship with others? When we begin to probe the mysteries of relationship, we recognize that the self is fundamental. We behave as we do with each other because of what drives us individually. The psychologist, concerned with behavior and selfhood, takes up the search in our understanding of the human mind: mental and emotional aspects.

Theologians, in turn, are concerned with the human spirit and the study of God. They probe the mysteries of the soul, or the very essence of humanity, and how we relate to the world within us, around us, and beyond us. The philosopher endeavors to apply reason to all these understandings. On and on it goes, this search to understand the complex creature called a human being.

To define humanity fully is difficult. But this we can say: We are made up of some of the properties found in all matter. We act and react physically much like other animals. Yet we appear to be distinct from the rest of life about us. The distinction is that we possess a consciousness of self, which is lacking in the rest of our environment. This consciousness is a keen awareness that we "are." It exhibits itself in our words, work, and feelings. That consciousness has three components as psychologists understand: the conscious (what we are aware of and can identify immediately), the subconscious (what we are only dimly aware of, just beyond the borders of consciousness), and the unconscious (what we are not aware of and yet affects us). All of these together make a single person and self.

Beyond this self-awareness, we have also become aware of a great "otherness," which we usually call "God." Indeed, this awareness of God, or God-consciousness, has been expressed in some form in the culture and understanding of every race of humankind. So we say that humans have an affinity with God. We are like God in his inner being. In order to understand this affinity and where it came from, we say that humans are created in the image of God. We possess a quality of life—a personality—that is both mental and spiritual. The search for this great "otherness" has been essential to our nature. If we could locate this great otherness, then we could communicate with it and influence it. Consequently, we have looked for this otherness in the sky, the earth, and the seas. We have endeavored to create the otherness with matter, making idols from the material world and trying to communicate with these gods of our own making.

Most humans have an innate sense of God. This takes on special meaning for Christians who believe that the Spirit of God dwells in them through the redemptive act of God in Christ. Consequently, Christians believe that the Holy Spirit intercedes on our behalf, even when we do not know how to pray as we should.

Our spirit communes with God in the experience of prayer. Our material body, however, plays a great part in preparing us for the experience and is, in part, the vehicle of expression. Prayer, then, is the dialogue of the human spirit communicating with the Spirit of God.

We know that God exists beyond the human person. Theology speaks of the immanence of God, his presence in and involvement with his world. Theology also speaks of the transcendence of God, that God exists apart from and is greater than the material universe. He is a God we can relate to and who wants to relate with us. Prayer is relational. We must let God be God in this relationship.

Who Is God?

We have defined prayer as a conversation between a human being and God. We have concluded that the totality of our being is active when we are praying. Yet we are but one participant in the act of prayer. We can observe humans with our senses. We can interpret our mental processes by observation and analysis, but what about God? How do we observe and analyze him? Is he real? We don't want to simply pretend to relate to someone who doesn't really exist.

Our purpose here is not to try to prove the existence of God. There are well-defined philosophical arguments for God's existence, such as the argument that the very design of the universe implies the existence of a designer, or that the goodness in the world implies a fountainhead of goodness. The proven law of cause and effect is frequently used as an argument for the existence of God: Just as every cause must have an effect, so must every effect have a cause. The effect is obvious: you and I, "the world and they that dwell therein." The cause is God. Perhaps the strongest and most practical argument for God's existence is, "I know there is a God because I know there is a God." The history of humankind corroborates this affirmation.

These time-honored "proofs" of God's existence, while helpful in establishing a reason for one's belief, are in themselves subject to the attack of pure logic. In fact, the basic conviction of the reality of God as the otherness in the prayer dialogue, although it is reasonable, cannot be founded upon sheer reason alone—but rather on faith. Indeed, the Bible is based on the premise that God exists. The Bible begins with "In the beginning God . . ." and never spends time proving this statement.

To understand prayer, it is not necessary to catch God in a test tube before we accept his reality. In order to understand and commune with God, we must first accept him just as we accept ourselves as persons who are different from the animals around us. In other words, knowing who we are as created in the image of God, we accept that God is who he is and that we may communicate with him.

Who, then, is this God with whom we converse in prayer? To begin with, God is not merely a cosmic blob or infinite nothingness. Nor is God a house detective, a little spy who watches for mistakes and punishes us when we sin. God is not simply synonymous with conscience. Moreover, God is not to be thought of as our projected ego, the development of all that we would like to be but can't, a figment of our imagination, a glorified shadow we choose to cast. God is not simply a grand old man like Santa Claus, who showers us with gifts at our asking. Nor is God an itinerant horse-and-buggy doctor, here today and gone tomorrow, the great Creator who made the world and then left it to its own workings.

God is a person. Humans are persons. A *person* is defined as "a being characterized by conscious apprehension, rationality, and a moral sense." God does not have a physical body; he doesn't need one. We, however, need a physical body to interact with the physical world around us. Remember that the physical body is not the person, but rather the external case that houses the person.

My (Chet's) family had all gathered near my mother's hospital room. She was in the last hours of her battle with leukemia. It was my turn to go into her room. She lay very still. As I approached her bed, she smiled. What do you say to your mother at her dying moment? "How are you, Mom?" I asked. She could barely whisper. I put my ear near her lips as she faintly replied, "I'm fine. I've never been better. The real Edith Tolson is alive and well. The body she lives in is falling apart. Soon I will have a new body for eternity." I'm sure she was referring to Paul's statement that the mortal will put on immortality (1 Cor. 15:54).

And so, when we pray, it is not our physical body that is essentially communicating in the dialogue, but rather the spirit personhood within us. We are permanent personalities dwelling in temporary bodies. The real person within is a spirit, a personal, living spirit.

This personal living spirit communicates with the person of God in prayer. For God, too, is Spirit. Not something unreal and totally other but a personal, living Spirit. As recorded in John 4:24, "God is Spirit, and those who worship Him must worship in spirit and truth." God is not in need of a physical body, because his existence is not merely within a material environment of time and space. Scripture does record that he "emptied Himself, taking the form of a bond-servant, being made in the [physical] likeness of men" (Phil. 2:7 NASB). On this occasion, God, too, was housed in human form in the person of Jesus Christ. He hungered, wept, slept, and died. And rose from the dead. God is a personality. God does possess those qualities of personhood that make us who we are, and thus we can commune with him.

God is a kindred being, or, as Jesus said, "When you pray, say, 'Our Father.'" It is this concept of God as a personality with likes and dislikes, with a will and a purpose, who feels and can hurt, that gives meaning to the experience of prayer. Prayer is conversation of a person with a person: the real self of humanity and the person of God.

These conversations may take many forms but the same dynamics occur. Here are some examples:

Our nation had just experienced our most horrific attack in our history on September 11, 2001. Evil terrorists had invaded our skies with hijacked airplanes and bombed our national center for business in New York City, and our Pentagon in Washington, D.C., which houses our national defense center, and another plane was headed for Washington, D.C., to bomb our center of government. Thousands of innocent citizens were killed. Property damage beyond comprehension was caused. Our nation was angry, shocked, sad, and devastated. As soon as the news of the tragedy spread to the citizenry, the leaders of our nation were calling for people to stop and pray. And we did. No fewer than nine out of ten Americans turned to religion and prayer to cope.[1] Shortly after the tragic event, our president called for a special prayer service at the National Cathedral in Washington, D.C. The leaders of all branches of government and national influence were present. Rev. Billy Graham, the country's "national chaplain," led the people in the cathedral and millions listening on television and radio in prayer. He implored God to help us, guide us, and give us peace. We were talking together with God.

During the September 11 attacks, one of the terrorist-hijacked airplanes heading for our nation's capital was forced by the assault of the passengers on the aircraft to crash in Pennsylvania. This prevented more national devastation. One of the heroes among the passengers had made several calls from the aircraft to his wife using his cellular telephone. He was talking to the phone operator; in his last conversation with her, as he described their plans to subdue the terrorists, he asked her to join him in the Lord's Prayer. They were talking with God.

Someone in Colorado entered the bedroom of a teenage child and kidnapped her. The family, neighbors, and nation were deeply distressed. Her father and mother appeared on national television and called on people everywhere to join them in prayer. We were communicating to God together.

Every Sunday morning, and at other times, all over the world, people gather together for personal enrichment, strength, thanksgiving, and divine guidance. The settings vary widely but the high point of the gathering we call worship is prayer. In whatever fashion it may be structured, prayer involves people talking and communicating with God.

In time of crisis—whether physical, emotional, or financial, during times of threatening change, relational frustration, or fear—we pray. We talk with God!

Prayer is a common thing. Prayer is natural. Prayer is basic to our well-being and happiness.

We talk with God just as we talk with one another. Sometimes it may be audible and sometimes silent. Most of the time, when I (Chet) am praying alone, I make no sounds and generally do not move my lips. But my mind is active and I am aware of what I am saying. The responses I receive from God, with whom I am talking, are likewise clear and understandable. I talk in the same language and with words that I use in ordinary conversation. Some people claim a gift of prayer language or speaking in tongues. They witness that it is helpful to them in communicating with God. Many do not possess this gift. However, we can all communicate with God and converse with him fully and confidently. We know that God hears us and are assured that he will answer and direct us.

We don't really need a whole lot of knowledge about prayer or prayer techniques. What we need to do is practice it. The more we pray, the more clearly we will understand it and prosper from it. Emerson once said, "No one ever prayed without learning something." This is undoubtedly true.

So talk with God and no breath will be lost; walk with God and no strength will be lost; wait on God and no time will be lost. Talking, listening, waiting, moving with God—that is prayer and it is powerful. So begin now—pray!

5

What Happens When We Pray?

A popular plaque reads, "Prayer changes things." This saying is found in many sizes and designs in many homes and is a source of inspiration to many. However, it is not entirely true. It implies that if we pray, God will answer our requests in the way we desire, even if it means that natural things will change. This may indeed occur—but not necessarily so.

A story is told about two boys who attended Sunday school, where they had been taught to pray. They were scheduled to go on an overnight camping trip. The day before the trip was to begin, it started to rain, not a sprinkle but a downpour. The camp leaders got word to the boys that if it continued to rain all day, the trip would be canceled. The rain kept falling all day into the evening. The situation became grave for the boys. They decided to pray that the rain would stop. It didn't. It rained all that night and the following day. The camping trip was a complete washout. The boys were puzzled. Their simple faith seemed destroyed. Had they not prayed to God? Look what happened!

Their young minds may not have known it, but they were wrestling with a serious theological problem. They shared their doubts and confusion with a much wiser person who reminded them that while they were praying for the rain to stop, farmers were praying for the rain to fall because of drought conditions. It was explained to them that rain is a natural phenomenon. God, in his creative wisdom, has made it that way. We cannot always expect God to alter his laws of nature to please us. God is not a divine furniture mover rearranging his universe in order to make us comfortable and happy.

We can all relate to this story. In matters with much more serious consequences than a washed-out camping trip, the principle remains the same. Prayer may not always change things; rather, through prayer we are often changed in relation to things. Whether external events are changed or not, prayer always changes us.

This does not mean that God cannot or does not alter his laws of the universe in response to prayer. Sometimes, he does precisely that. But generally, God operates within his universal laws. This would include the laws of nature, physiology, psychology, and theology.

When we pray we are changed and act more in harmony with the divine plan. When a person is changed, as a result of prayer, the conditions surrounding him seem to change as well. It is all within God's ordered plan. Through prayer we find ourselves more in tune with the divine purpose for our lives. In this God-human encounter, we come out of our dialogue enabled to cope, to overcome, to move ahead, and to live victoriously. What an enormous change occurs within us when we pray. We often kneel so weak, yet rise full of power.

From these prayer experiences, many good things happen in our lives.

Prayer Helps Us Rise above Loneliness

Loneliness is a serious problem for many people. Loneliness makes us feel as though we are isolated and no one really cares about us. Some have said that loneliness is at the root of many emotional problems that people experience. For example, in a study of 1,132 persons living in the greater San Francisco Bay area, Susan Nolen-Hoeksema and Cheryl Ahrens of the psychology department at the University of Michigan examined characteristics of these people, and then predicted whether or not they were depressed.[1] Of all the characteristics they measured, loneliness was the strongest predictor of depression. When they divided their sample into three age groups (25 to 35, 45 to 55, and 65 to 75), this was true for all of the groups, especially the older age groups.

One reason for being lonely is feeling that we don't belong. We have lost our centering. So many people have "no hills of home." They wander to and fro, seeking something or someone with whom they can relate. They look for love in all the wrong places. A harsh example of this is the vast group of runaway youth who escape to the big cities where they are even lonelier. They may turn to chemicals and get hooked on the drugs, because this at least temporarily relieves them of this terrible feeling. But when they sober up, they feel even lonelier. Their primary purpose in life begins to revolve around finding the drugs, paying for the drugs, and hiding from those who might discover what they are doing. This frequently results in physical illness, emotional breakdown, criminal behavior, and sometimes death.

The pathway to this degeneration can often be traced back to loneliness. We all seek to have companionship, relationships, and a sense of belonging.

We believe that we can rise above our loneliness by relating to God. Prayer is a way for us to touch God and a way for God to touch us. This may be one of the most important axioms of life: to know and believe that whatever we do, wherever we go, however we feel, we are never alone. The psalmist says,

Where can I go from Your Spirit?
Or where can I flee from Your presence?
If I ascend into heaven, You are there;
If I make my bed in hell, behold, You are there.
If I take the wings of the morning,
And dwell in the uttermost parts of the sea,
Even there Your hand shall lead me,
And Your right hand shall hold me.

Psalm 139:7–10

God is always there!

This may be difficult to believe and even harder to live by. Sometimes the very "bigness of God" seems so awesome that we cannot tune in with him in conversation. As we view the complexities of nature and the amazing world around us, it may be difficult to believe that God would have the time, much less the interest, to talk with us.

For example, our earth's sun, which we take for granted as it furnishes the light and heat for us to live by, is ninety-three million miles away from our earth. Its light takes eight minutes to reach us. Yet every day it's there. The light from Sirius, the brightest star in the heavens, takes eight years to reach us. Someone has calculated that light from Nebula 287 takes eight million years to reach us. No wonder the psalmist said,

When I consider Your heavens, the work of Your fingers,
The moon and the stars, which You have ordained,
What is man that You are mindful of him,
And the son of man that You visit him?

Psalm 8:3–4

Any scientist who spends time looking through a microscope at a thumbprint is baffled by the complex and highly organized pattern that is present. All of nature seems to say that there is nothing too great for the Creator to accomplish and nothing too small for him to attend to. In prayer we say, "Our Father," and he immediately responds, "Yes, my child." Prayer makes us aware that God is with us. He is our ever-present friend who is "closer than a brother" (Prov. 18:24). This confidence rises to a crescendo when we sing the old hymn "What a Friend We Have in Jesus."

Loneliness and being alone are not always the same. We have all known people who were alone a great deal of the time but remained happy, vital, and at peace. We have often heard about people who are in the midst of a crowd constantly but are very lonely. Celebrities sometimes share this feeling of distance from others and a sense of emptiness. Being alone means "being apart from everyone else."

Loneliness means feeling isolated or unfriended. This is a serious problem. Jesus spoke to this when he said in John 14:1, "Let not your heart be troubled; you believe in God, believe also in Me." In prayer we actualize our faith by communicating with God. In that experience we are lifted above loneliness. There's healing power in prayer.

Prayer Helps Us Overcome Fear

Loneliness can lead to fear and fear can sometimes lead to serious illness. Many medical doctors would agree that a large percentage of disease seems to be rooted in anxiety and fear. Fear is a root cause for many of our negative and depressive thoughts. One study of five hundred people indicated that all together they had about seven thousand distinguishable fears. The group doing the research said that people are born with two basic fears: the fear of falling and the fear of loud noises. All the other fears seemed to be acquired. Think of that. Five hundred people burdened with 6,998 unnatural and useless fears.

Some anxiety is a God-given blessing. When faced with a crisis, we intuitively flee or fight. This is our built-in survival system. However, many people carry fear to such a point that their physical and emotional health is hindered.

Fear and severe anxiety are well-known predictors of sudden death from heart attack. On January 17, 1994, an earthquake struck near Los Angeles at 4:31 A.M. Millions of people were suddenly awakened with intense fright. Within one hour of the earthquake, the number of persons who died from sudden cardiac death increased to five times what was expected.[2] The same phenomenon of increased sudden death and heart attack was noted following the Iraqi missile attacks in Israel.[3] Evidence also exists that chronic anxiety may increase the risk of sudden cardiac death, and that even low-to-moderate levels of anxiety may be capable of increasing that risk.[4]

A young woman was diagnosed with agoraphobia at age twenty-three. This fear usually begins in early adulthood and is more common in women than men. This woman has lived with panic disorder for nearly thirty years. She experiences fear of being with people, driving a car, going shopping, and being in a crowded place. *Agoraphobia* literally means "fear of the marketplace." At times she has been unable to go outside her house even to the mailbox. She is overcome with an overwhelming feeling of terror. She cannot predict when an attack will occur. She even develops intense anxiety between episodes, worrying when and where the next one will occur. Her social life, workplace experiences, and travel plans are all affected by this fear.

She has tried many things to cure her anxiety, including doctor-prescribed drug therapy, cognitive and behavioral counseling, supportive group therapy, yoga and other Eastern exercises, Western exercises, Christian religious rituals, and relaxation techniques through music. All of these healing agents have helped her to become a healthier person, but none have completely cured her agoraphobia.

Nevertheless, she says that prayer is her biggest help in allowing her to cope. She says that if she stays connected with the present and focuses on the here and now, she can overcome her anxiety. She cannot focus on the future and anticipate the unknown. She cannot focus on the past, which brings up guilt, faults, and other past anxiety. When she "lets go and lets God," her life maintains the best equilibrium for her.

Prayer is her greatest support.

As we are overtaken with fear, we should immediately "let go and let God." God becomes our primary defense system.

We should let God be our bodyguard. He is always with us and always sovereign.

The woman with agoraphobia says that she has noticed two things when she has anxiety attacks. First, she describes herself as "involved in me." Prayer lifts her out of herself into God's presence and a grander plan for her life.

Second, when she is experiencing the anxiety, she cannot really truly trust God to stop the anxiety. That's understandable, because at that time she is experiencing severe doubt. Faith becomes the key. Living in an abiding faith may become our chief defense. The writer of Hebrews says, "Faith is the substance of things hoped for, the evidence of things not seen" (Heb. 11:1). The psalmist reminded, "Cast your burden on the LORD, and He shall sustain you; He shall never permit the righteous to be moved" (Ps. 55:22). He also wrote, "For He shall give His angels charge over you, to keep you in all your ways" (Ps. 91:11). Hear what John says in the New Testament: "Perfect love casts out fear" (1 John 4:18).

The best definition we have of God is that "God is love" (1 John 4:8). God (because he is love) casts out our fears. We tap into that source of love when we pray.

Our part is to believe. God's part is to enable us to rise above the fear. His love for us does that. God loves you! Our love for one another is the actualization of God's love for us. Love moves us out of self-centeredness into a healthy external relationship with others. This continuation of God's love for us and our love for him and for one another is a way we may overcome fear.

Fear imprisons. Love liberates.

Fear paralyzes. Love empowers.

Fear disheartens. Love encourages.

Fear sickens. Love heals.

Fear makes us useless. Love makes us productive.

We tune in to that perfect love in prayer.

Prayer Helps Give Us Power

Power is an important word today. It means "the ability to achieve." Power is not unique to our generation. We hear about horsepower, candlepower, cosmic power, and other forms of energy to make things happen. When man threw his first stone or pulled his first bow he was using the power of stored energy. Today, we have successfully harnessed the power of water, heat, wind, electricity, and the atom. We use energy stored in the earth's crust, such as oil, coal, uranium, and other elements as a source of power. Now we are applying the technologies of linking computers and new materials from the ocean and outer space, all as new energy bases.

Another kind of energy has always existed—spiritual power. It is the linkage of humans with God. Spiritual energy cannot be measured by calories, kilowatts, or horsepower. This power is measured by a person's ability to achieve higher levels of morality, peace, wellness, and love.

This spiritual energy is as pervasive as solar energy or radiation. Like any other form of energy, it must be harnessed in order to be used. The TV in your home must be turned on and tuned in for you to see your favorite program. We must be turned on to God and tuned into his infinite spiritual energy in order to receive the power he has promised us. This is what prayer is about.

You receive power through prayer and greater ability to achieve God's plan in your life. We call this "prayer power."

Prayer Helps Us Develop Self-Esteem

Lack of self-esteem may be the causative factor for many illnesses, social inadequacies, and vocational limitations. The person who has little self-worth may make unsatisfactory relationships and settle for a life of failure at work and home. Feelings of low self-esteem during early childhood have been shown to predict depression and suicidal tendencies in early adulthood.[5] Low self-esteem has also been shown to predict problem eating and other multiple health-compromising behaviors such as smoking.[6] A study of women following surgery that resulted in damage to the facial nerve and consequent facial paralysis discovered that low self-esteem was the strongest predictor of emotional distress among all the characteristics examined.[7] Finally, low self-esteem has been shown to predict violence and physical aggression in both teens and adults,[8] and may even predict acts of terrorism.[9]

Lack of self-esteem may be the result of a person's focus. Recall that the writer in Proverbs wrote: "For as he thinks within himself, so he is" (Prov. 23:7 NASB). What do we think about ourselves? Do we see our bodies as unattractive? Don't depreciate your body because it is not like what you see in another person. You have no need to look like the model on TV. If you are older, don't look at your body as though it was twenty years younger. Thank God for your body, and make it the best that it can be for your particular age. Commit yourself to a healthy diet and exercise regimen that you can maintain.

Remember what Paul said to the church at Corinth: "Do you not know that your body is the temple of the Holy Spirit who is in you, whom you have from God, and you are not your own?" (1 Cor. 6:19). How can we have a low self-image if God is dwelling in us? Whatever condition we are in or however we see ourselves, we really are VIPs (very important persons) because the God of the universe dwells in us, through Jesus Christ our Lord.

And what is really exciting is that you may constantly communicate with him if you wish. You don't need to talk to God's voice message system, go through his secretary, take a number and stand in line, or wait for him to call you back. The instant you begin your prayer God is there immediately, saying, "Yes, my child." We don't need to let low self-esteem destroy us. We are made in the image of the God who made the universe. This realization will give us enormous self-worth. Even more important, however, is acting on that realization.

There was a young woman who had epilepsy. When she experienced a seizure and went into convulsions, she suffered a great loss of self-esteem. She and her family were embarrassed if this occurred in public. She was under good medical supervision and took her prescriptions regularly. She decided to do more to relieve her feelings of low self-worth.

She set a goal to live above her disability. She had a great love for animals and discovered she had a skill in caring for them. She opened an adoption center for lost or forsaken small domestic pets. This put her in contact with people who needed a family pet and took her focus off of herself and her physical problems. She developed a daily routine around her service to others. To this she added prayer.

She said that prayer became the most natural and helpful thing she did. As she prayed about her animals and homes for their adoption, she realized she had an important role in life. She continued on her medications, but the doctor decreased the dosage. She has not had a major seizure in two years. She feels that empowering her self-worth by taking action, getting her attention off of her own physical problem, and communicating regularly with God, the divine source of everything, resulted in her being healed from her illness. As she says, "I still have the epilepsy; I am not cured, but I am healed from its debilitations." Prayer has helped to generate in her a new sense of self-esteem.

Prayer Helps Relieve Guilt

Many of us go through life with the burden of guilt from yesterday's thoughts, words, and deeds. We *should* feel responsible for bad things we have done in the past, and we should make every effort to make restitution, when we can. But, we should be careful not to let past sins destroy us. Excessive guilt can increase anxiety and lead to depression, especially in those with chronic illness,[10] as well as cause changes in the physical body that make it more susceptible to disease and less likely to recover.[11]

I (Harold) once had a patient named Bob whose sixteen-year-old son committed suicide. Bob felt incredibly guilty because he thought that he should have picked up on the danger signs that his son was displaying. Nearly ten years after the event, he remained chronically depressed and suffering, convinced that he deserved this suffering and certain that nothing I did would be effective in relieving it. Driven by this guilt, he gained nearly a hundred pounds and developed severe high blood pressure and asthmatic lung problems.

Guilt not only causes emotional distress but also may be a symptom of it. A diagnosis of clinical depression depends on the presence of certain symptoms, one of which is guilt and preoccupation with sin or wrongdoing. Again, we're talking about pathological guilt here. Guilt does serve a very useful purpose in constraining our actions, and those without guilt are often found in prisons.

Although religion may point out our guilt and make us feel guilty at times, religion may also have an enormous role in relieving guilt. Guilt is associated with the word *sin*, which means "missing the mark." We are constantly reminded by our thoughts, words, and deeds that we miss the mark. We all sin! The Bible says, "All have sinned and fall short of the glory of God" (Rom. 3:23).

A young man ran into his pastor's office and screamed, "My guilt is driving me nuts!" And it was. This gentleman, like everyone else, desperately needs forgiveness for his transgressions.

The psalmist says, "For You, LORD, are good, and ready to forgive" (Ps. 86:5). Again, we have this assurance:

> Bless the LORD, O my soul;
> And all that is within me, bless His holy name!
> Bless the LORD, O my soul,
> And forget not all His benefits:
> Who forgives all your iniquities,
> Who heals all your diseases.
>
> Psalm 103:1–3

And again: "As far as the east is from the west, so far has He removed our transgressions from us" (Ps. 103:12).

The New Testament is centered on this theme of forgiveness and the hope that gives us peace and serenity within. It reaches its climax in John 3:16: "For God so loved the world that He gave His only begotten Son, that whoever believes in Him should not perish but have everlasting life."

Prayer is a way to tap into this hope and assurance. "If we confess our sins, He is faithful and just to forgive us our sins and to cleanse us from all unrighteousness" (1 John 1:9).

Forgiveness will set us free from the bondage of guilt. And with this freedom we may move into a new paradigm for living. Paul expressed it well in his letter to the church at Philippi: "Forgetting those things which are behind and reaching forward to those things which are ahead, I press on toward the goal for the prize of the upward call of God in Christ Jesus" (Phil. 3:13–14).

God's forgiveness enables us to rise above our guilt and move on. We receive this forgiveness through faith, and faith is actualized through prayer. In this experience of being forgiven, we are able to reach out and forgive others.

On the other hand, studies have shown that people who are unforgiving and hostile suffer greater emotional and physical problems. The cover story of a recent edition of the *Cleveland Clinic Heart Advisor,* published by one of the most prestigious medical centers in the nation, focused on how hostility may have serious harmful effects on the heart.

Dr. Redford Williams and his wife, Virginia, have written a book entitled *Anger Kills.*[12] In it they describe the many scientific studies that show how anger increases the risk of developing coronary artery disease, high blood pressure, and of experiencing a heart attack or a stroke. Truly, anger does kill, and is perhaps one reason why Jesus said during his Sermon on the Mount, "But I tell you that anyone who is angry with his brother will be subject to judgment" (Matt. 5:22 NIV)—judgment both in this world and the next. Prayer gives us a new perspective on situations so that we can release our anger and forgive our brother.

Hostility and unforgiveness are serious problems.

Even business recognizes this. A successful real estate board had a speaker address anger management. He said that anger control is part and parcel of good business. Anger will lose business. All evidence says that anger is harmful for the physical body, harmful for the mind, harmful for the spirit, and harmful for the pocketbook.

On the other hand, people who forgive have less stress. Research suggests that:

- People who forgive and forget enjoy better physical and emotional health than their grudge-holding peers.
- The grudge-holders tend to get angry and fearful. Each emotion can cause heart rate and blood pressure to rise.
- Over time, this can lead to heart attack, stroke, and other ailments.

Accepting God's forgiveness of our transgressions against him, we should reach out to forgive people who may have harmed us. This whole notion of loving, forgiving, and showing mercy may seem contrary to the principle that survival is enhanced by defeating and annihilating one's enemies. That seems to be the law of the jungle, "the survival of the fittest." We live by a higher standard. Humanity survives best when hostility is seen as a source of illness and forgiveness a source of wellness.

Paul wrote to the Christians at Colossae, "Bearing with one another, and forgiving one another, if anyone has a complaint against another; even as Christ forgave you, so you also must do" (Col. 3:13).

Prayer is the proven tool through which we experience God's forgiveness for our transgressions. Prayer is the proven tool through which we are convicted to forgive another person and are guided on how we may actualize that forgiveness. There is enormous healing value in the power of forgiveness. Being forgiven by God and forgiving one another are the alternate beats of the same great heart of love.

What Happens When We Pray?

In summary, when we pray we are changed. Prayer helps us rise above our loneliness and overcome our fears. It enables us to accomplish so much more in our lives, which contributes to our self-esteem and sense of well-being. Prayer also gives us greater self-confidence because it connects us to an omnipotent Friend who loves us and wants to help us. Finally, prayer helps us to release our anger and resentment by enabling us to forgive others and to accept forgiveness ourselves, which neutralizes excessive guilt that can only damage us physically, emotionally, and spiritually. Prayer does a great deal for us in all phases of our lives.

6

GRACE AND PRAYER

*P*rayer is in style! One of the most common practices among human beings is prayer. One of the most important subjects you could read and learn about is prayer.

In the year 2001 the world population was 6,137,000,000. Approximately 850,000,000 claimed to be atheists or nonreligious, and that number is dubious. (A common expression during wartime is "There are no atheists in foxholes." In other words, when push comes to shove and they are trapped with no place to go, even atheists call on God for help.) Prayer is part of the belief system of the other five billion or so people on earth. Here's how they were grouped in the year 2001:

Christians—2,130,000,000
Muslims—1,300,000,000
Hindus—900,000,000
Buddhists—360,000,000

New religionists—140,000,000
Tribal religionists—101,000,000
Sikhs—23,000,000
Jews—14,000,000
All other religionists—187,000,000

All of these people have some form of religious belief in some form of prayer. In actual human practices, prayer ranks with the necessities for survival such as water, food, shelter, health, security, government, and natural resources. Prayer is an important subject for our existence on earth. Add to that the hope of life eternal, where prayer is a vital factor.

As this chapter was being written, the word *prayer* was one of the most repeated words by the national media. During a two-week period, *prayer* was used more than any other word. Here are some examples:

Two little girls, five and six years old, were abducted, sexually abused, and murdered. Until they were found, the nation was praying for their safe return. When they were found, people were praying that the murderers would be found and justice would prevail. At the memorial service, the people were praying that the families would be comforted and strengthened.

Nine miners were trapped 240 feet below the surface of the ground in a watery shaft. The rescuers drilled for seventy-four hours with what were called one in a million odds that they were at the right spot. During that anxious time the miners later said that they prayed for their survival. Family, friends, and the nation prayed for their rescue. As each miner was returned to the ground surface, everyone involved offered a prayer of thanksgiving for this miracle. The sign at the fast-food restaurant near the mine site read: "Thank God for the rescue."

Pope John Paul II said prayers for nearly one million people attending the youth day celebration in Toronto, Canada. Thirty-three percent of the population of the world claims to be Christian and 50 percent of those are Roman Catholics. Here was their earthly leader, telling all who were listening to pray.

The historic definition of *prayer* is "communion with God." It implies that God is a person, able and willing to hear us. He has created the universe and still governs it. He is not restricted by his own laws. In his governance, he may cooperate with the laws of nature or he may move outside these laws. When we are praying we must respect God's own integrity. Let God be God! Through prayer, God can influence a person to action even more than a human may influence his fellowman. Prayer becomes for us a key to living.

Prayer is a natural expression of our spiritual feelings. We do not enter prayer out of our own righteousness. It is through grace that we may enter into this conversation. *Grace* simply means "unmerited favor." We don't bring holiness into the dialogue, God does. Yet he allows us to enter into his sovereign presence. Hundreds of years before Jesus lived on the earth, died for our transgression, and gave us hope for righteousness, the psalmist, speaking on the subject of the grace of God, declared:

> The LORD is gracious and full of compassion,
> Slow to anger and great in mercy.
> The LORD is good to all,
> And His tender mercies are over all His works.
>
> Psalm 145:8–9

Common Grace and Prayer

This "common grace" of God toward all his creation runs like a golden thread throughout the history of humankind. God cares for each of us and in that caring he welcomes us into his presence. Some Old Testament references seem to suggest that acceptable prayer to God could be offered by the righteous only. That is, only those who had forsaken sin were authorized to approach God in prayer. The writer of Proverbs says, "One who turns away his ear from hearing the law, even his prayer is an abomination" (Prov. 28:9). Earlier we find: "The LORD is far from the wicked, but He hears the prayers of the righteous" (Prov. 15:29).

The Grace of Our Lord Jesus Christ and Prayer

Does that mean that only good and righteous people can pray? No. It means that to receive what God has for us we must be open to receive and to be connected to him. Our unrighteousness is superceded by God's grace for us. In the New Testament Paul sums up this hope in his message to the church at Rome:

> While we were still sinners, Christ died for us. Much more then, having now been justified by His blood, we shall be saved from wrath through Him. For if when we were enemies we were reconciled to God through the death of His Son, much more, having been reconciled, we shall be saved by His life. And not only that, but we also rejoice in God through our Lord Jesus Christ, through whom we have now received this reconciliation.
>
> Romans 5:8–11

As a result of this reconciliation through Jesus Christ, we are capable of meeting God in prayer. Prayer is relational. We come to the table of prayer bringing our sins, forgiven through our faith in Christ, and God, who is totally righteous, is able to hear our prayers in the light of our redemption. Does that mean that God only hears the prayers of the redeemed? No, because God is the Father of all humankind. He created all in his image. It does mean that the prayer of the redeemed becomes more intimate and personal because the "praying field" is more level. This does not make the redeemed arrogant, but grateful. Remembering that this grace through Jesus Christ is available to all humankind, the Christian should not point a finger at the non-Christian in judgment and condemnation. It means that the Christian should live out and extend the message of hope. "For by grace you have been saved through faith, and that not of yourselves; it is the gift of God" (Eph. 2:8).

Simply stated, here is the formula for our righteousness:

1. We are saved from our unrighteousness through faith. We have to believe that!
2. It is not because of what we have done but what Christ has done. We have to affirm that!
3. It is the gift of God. We have to accept it! (A gift is not truly a gift unless it is accepted.)

That's the message for the whole human race. Implementing this formula we truly have intimate access to God. This becomes the power drive for all Christians to "go into all the world and preach the gospel to every creature" (Mark 16:15). This Great Commission of Jesus is the Christian's motive for evangelism.

The grace of our Lord Jesus Christ truly adds a great dimension for the prayer life of anyone. *Grace* is a marvelous word. It comes from the Greek word *karis,* which means that we are treated by God as good even though we don't deserve it. This grace is our personal ticket to have a visit with God. It is available for all at any time.

If we were conducting a poll of what is most important for living, prayer might not rank in the top category, but it should. Remember, in prayer we are talking with the same God who made the world and all that is in it.

When you think about prayer this way, it becomes a treasure for us to enjoy and practice. In this book our intention is not to merely explain prayer but to encourage the development of prayer habits so that prayer becomes a regular part of our daily lives. Prayer should not merely be used in those moments of crisis or when we feel the urge to pray.

Prayer should not be something we do or practice only in a religious environment. In fact, Paul urges us to "pray without ceasing" (1 Thess. 5:17). Obviously, even a monk living in a monastery for prayer does things other than pray. His physical and emotional life requires that. What Paul seems to be saying is that we should always be tuned in so that God may speak to us. It's a matter of attitude. If our primary attitude is to do the will of God then we will be, in that sense, praying constantly.

Habitual Prayer

However, there are those special moments when we put other things aside and have a good visit with God. It is these habitual visits that we want to develop.

Many of us can recall a parent, a grandparent, or someone we knew who prayed with regularity. We remember their dedication to prayer; when we think of them we automatically think of prayer.

People who develop a daily habit of prayer become more comfortable in these visits with God, as they experience them. Prayer becomes their way of life, their lifestyle.

People change lifestyles often. In many cases it is for the better. We cannot recall a person of prayer—someone who made it a vital part of his or her daily life to pray—who decided one day to quit praying. Of course, physical and emotional changes may alter their prayer habits. People's belief systems or theological perspectives may change, but they keep on praying if they have really developed a meaningful experience of daily conversation with God.

I (Chet) recall a woman who made prayer her daily routine. Her family and friends knew her as "a woman of prayer." She became the victim of Alzheimer's disease. She soon was unable to communicate with her family and friends. She seemed uninterested in anything occurring around her. One day, she and her husband were in an automobile accident. She suffered a brain concussion and went into a coma. Her daughter and husband were by her bedside when suddenly she looked up and smiled and said simply, "Everything is going to be all right." She then went back into a coma. Her husband and daughter said she had the facial expression and countenance that they remembered before when she was praying. They felt it was prayer, at that moment, that stimulated her cognitive response, "Everything is going to be all right."

I (Harold) have had patients with late stage Alzheimer's disease who could not care for themselves or recognize family members, but who could recall spiritual aspects of their lives to the finest detail. These people were typically deeply religious when younger. One example is an eighty-year-old man who, I was told, had been a deacon in his church for many years and was a powerful man of prayer. Although he could remember almost nothing about his present or past, he could readily tell me every aspect of his conversion experience over fifty years before. He beamed as he recalled that experience. Although nearly all of his past experience had been wiped out by this terrible disease, the one thing that remained was his faith that had been finely tuned during his younger years with regular, daily prayer.

Many people who pray regularly will say, "I couldn't live without it." Prayer is that instrument that connects us with God.

William W. Walford wrote a poem in 1842 that a few years later was put to music by William Bradbury, and describes beautifully this experience:

> Sweet hour of prayer,
> Sweet hour of prayer,
> That calls me from a world of care
> And bids me at my Father's throne
> Make all my wants and wishes known!
> In seasons of distress and grief,
> My soul has often found relief,
> And oft escaped the tempter's snare
> By thy return, sweet hour of prayer.
>
> Sweet hour of prayer,
> Sweet hour of prayer,
> Thy wings shall my petition bear
> To Him whose truth and faithfulness
> Engage the waiting soul to bless:
> And since He bids me seek His face,
> Believe His word and trust His grace,
> I'll cast on Him my every care,
> And wait for Thee, sweet hour of prayer.

Those are inspiring words of what prayer can do for us. (Read that familiar hymn, over and over, line by line. It may really pull prayer together for you.)

Prayer in Heaven

Through God's grace we have been created.

So God created man in His own image; in the image of God He created him; male and female He created them.

Genesis 1:27

Through God's grace we have been saved.

But God, who is rich in mercy, because of His great love with which He loved us, even when we were dead in trespasses, made us alive together with Christ (by grace you have been saved), and raised us up together, and made us sit together in heavenly places in Christ Jesus, that in the ages to come He might show the exceeding riches of His grace in his kindness toward us in Christ Jesus. For by grace you have been saved through faith, and that not of yourselves; it is the gift of God, not of works, lest anyone should boast.

Ephesians 2:4–9

Through God's grace we are sustained in this life.

And lest I should be exalted above measure by the abundance of the revelations, a thorn in the flesh was given to me, a messenger of Satan to buffet me, lest I be exalted above measure. Concerning this thing I pleaded with the Lord three times that it might depart from me. And He said to me, "My grace is sufficient for you, for My strength is made perfect in weakness." Therefore most gladly I will rather boast in my infirmities, that the power of Christ may rest upon me. Therefore I take pleasure in infirmities, . . . in distresses, for Christ's sake. For when I am weak, then I am strong.

2 Corinthians 12:7–10

Through God's grace we have eternal life.

My sheep hear My voice, and I know them, and they follow Me.
And I give them eternal life, and they shall never perish; neither
shall anyone snatch them out of my hand.

John 10:27–28

Through the grace of God, we live, abide in this life, and are
saved for life eternal. Grace allows us to pray, and prayer is a
means of grace. Through prayer we have access to the throne
of God. Prayer becomes the language for our visits with God
and prayer becomes the language of heaven. As we pray in this
life, we are honing our language skills for heaven.

Heaven is where God dwells. Heaven is where, through the
grace of our Lord Jesus Christ, we will live forever. According
to a recent *Newsweek* poll, 76 percent of Americans believe in
heaven. Seventy-one percent think it is an actual place. Where
it is, how big it is, or what is its setting is of no real importance.
Heaven is a spiritual experience where we will enjoy life forever.
To be ready to communicate with God, whose dwelling place
heaven is, it is to our advantage to make a habit of communing
with God in this earthly life. When we reach that other side
for our life eternal, we will feel at home. We shall see Christ in
person without the handicap of space and time. As Mrs. Frank
A. Breck wrote in her hymn:

> Face to face with Christ, my Savior,
> Face to face—what will it be,
> When with rapture I behold Him,
> Jesus Christ who died for me?
>
> Only faintly now I see Him,
> With the darkened veil between,
> But a blessed day is coming,
> When His glory shall be seen.
>
> What rejoicing in His presence,
> When are banished grief and pain;
> When the crooked ways are straightened,
> And the dark things shall be plain.

Face to face—oh, blissful moment!
Face to face—to see and know;
Face to face with my Redeemer,
Jesus Christ who loves me so.

Face to face. I shall behold Him,
Far beyond the starry sky;
Face to face in all His glory,
I shall see Him by and by!

The grace of God makes this all possible. Faith makes this real
for each human being. Prayer actuates that faith.

7

FAITH AND PRAYER

A business person starts praying but keeps thinking about that deal about to happen. A professional person begins to pray but the thoughts about his patient or client take over. A homemaker is trying to pray but the needs of family, meals, and housework crowd out thoughts about God. The student would like to pray but his or her busy academic life and social demands take over. One of the problems involved in praying is keeping our thoughts centered on what we are doing and saying. It is especially true for those just beginning the practice of prayer. The longer one prays and the greater the regularity, wandering and disturbing thoughts become less of a problem.

Why is it sometimes difficult to pray? It may be one of several things. For example:

1. We find prayer boring.
2. We feel like we're merely talking to ourselves.

3. We doubt that there is really "someone out there" listening.
4. We haven't prepared ourselves for this visit with God.
5. We have a problem concentrating.
6. We don't have time for prayer.
7. We don't want to pray.

These are problems regarding prayer that all of us may have. They fall into three general categories:

1. Faith
2. Focus
3. Follow-through

Faith and Prayer

Prayer without faith is like an engine without a power source. Without faith prayer may be nothing more than a repetition of words. Without faith we bring nothing to the table for our visit with God. Jesus was emphatic in pointing out the importance of faith in the experience of prayer. He said, "Whatever things you ask when you pray, believe that you receive them, and you will have them" (Mark 11:24).

This same positive affirmation was an essential element in his healing. He would ask the people requesting healing if they believed he could heal them (Matt. 9:28). After the healing was completed, he would remind them that their faith had made them whole (Matt. 9:22). The very tradition and practice of prayer teaches us that faith is the primary requisite on our part.

What is faith? A good and clear answer is: Belief + Trust = Faith.

- *Belief* means to accept something as true. It is intellectual assent.

- *Trust* means to commit. To accept without assurance of outcome. To accept the integrity of another's word or action. Children may believe the parent is capable of catching them when they jump into their arms in the swimming pool. For the child to trust that the parent will catch him is faith. On the level of our relationship with God, faith is the knowledge and trust that he will catch us if we leap toward him and accept his will for our lives. To be willing to say yes to God's proposal is the secret of abundant living. Begin with belief in God and in the possibility of communication with him through prayer, add to that a willingness to accept God's terms whatever, and you have *faith*.
- The Book of Hebrews has what many might say is the classic definition of faith: "Faith is the substance of things hoped for, the evidence of things not seen" (Heb. 11:1).
  - Substance means the real or essential part.
  - Hope means the feeling that what is needed will happen.
  - Evidence is something that tends to prove.

In this classic definition, the Book of Hebrews seems to be literally saying that faith is the proof and assurance that the essential part of what we need will happen.

The difficulties that keep us from faith are rational and intellectual. Faith is rationality *plus*. Logic says *possibly, maybe,* or *probably.* Faith says *absolutely.*

You can manage your life, with God's grace, on that certitude! You can depend on life everlasting with that same certainty.

Science depends upon investigation, experiment, and testing. From this formula comes knowledge. Faith activates knowledge. Knowledge gets us started and faith is the ultimate wave that safely brings us in. Knowledge leads us to believe in something; faith leads us to live by Someone.

Faith is more than a theological tenet. When Paul said, "I have kept the faith" (2 Tim. 4:7), he was not merely saying that he had been obedient to a creed. He was testifying that faith had been the main drive of his spiritual experience. Faith is that inward certainty through which we may face the unknown. Faith is intuition touched by the divine spark of God. We don't create faith. We live by it. Faith is not something you have or don't have; faith is the outstretched hand of God to us to hold onto. In this confidence we are able to have a meaningful prayer experience. God doesn't need faith; he is the creator of faith. We need faith to have confidence that God is really there communicating with us—we accept the hand that he has extended toward us.

Harry was an engineer. He managed his life on fixed principles that worked. Harry was also an active church person. He and his wife, Esther, attended church regularly. Harry contributed much of his time and resources to his church, serving on the church board and as the chair of the building and grounds committee. With Harry at the helm, everything seemed to run well.

Harry, however, had trouble praying. He believed in "the top of his mind" that prayer was possible, but in the "bottom of his heart" he had a problem actually praying.

One Sunday the pastor preached on the subject of prayer. Harry listened and struggled in relating to all of this. Following the service, he and Esther were having brunch at one of their favorite restaurants. Suddenly Harry said, "What do you think of the pastor's sermon today?" Esther responded that she thought it was excellent. Harry responded, "I really don't know if I believe in prayer. Whenever I try to pray alone I seem to get nowhere. I almost feel like I'm talking to myself. I really wish I could pray more effectively." Esther responded, "Well, maybe it's a matter of faith, Harry," to which he responded, "What do you mean?"

Esther said, "Prayer is relational, and it's something like our relationship. You believe that I am your wife. You acknowledge that we have been living together and have children together. You believe I truly exist as your soul mate. But there's more to us than just belief. You trust me. You know that I will be there when you really need me. You trust that I will love you whatever we might need to face together. Harry, try bringing that element of trust to your prayer relationship with God. I'm sure God has been hearing your prayers and answering them even though you might feel you haven't been sure. Just let go and trust God. Add trust to your mental assent." Harry thanked Esther with a tear in his eye, which was pretty significant for Harry, the engineer.

That night, Harry sat alone in his firm desk chair and simply said, "God, I accept you are here and I will never doubt your presence again." That began a whole new dimension in Harry's life. Belief plus trust did it; that is faith. And faith gives prayer the lift we need to make it real and meaningful. Harry died a few years ago. But those years after he listened to Esther's wisdom were filled with spiritual joy and hope.

Much scientific research suggests that having a strong belief in the effectiveness of a treatment or therapy is extremely important in that therapy actually working. Harvard cardiologist Herbert Benson has comprehensively reviewed these findings in his book *Timeless Healing: The Power and Biology of Belief.*[1] As the subtitle suggests, there is solid evidence that faith (belief and trust) is key to many successful medical treatments.

Faith is commitment. As the hard drive is to a computer, so is commitment to the experience of prayer. Just as you get to trust people more when you get to know them, the more you commit to visits with God, the easier it is to trust him. This commitment becomes key in the *healing power of prayer.*

On March 15, 1988, I (Chet) was serving as assistant to Dr. Robert H. Schuller, founding pastor of the Crystal Cathedral in Garden Grove, California, home of the *Hour of Power* television program. As we had done on many other days, Dr. Harold Englund, also serving on the pastoral staff at the Crystal Cathedral, and I were taking a noontime two-mile walk around the beautiful church campus. I had my camera with me as I planned to take some pictures of the removal of some apartment complexes, for which I had administrative responsibility, to make room for our new family life center. As usual, Harold and I were talking vigorously as we walked.

Suddenly, I experienced a sharp pain in my chest. I told Dr. Englund of my discomfort. He had previously experienced some heart problems and told me to rest. After a few minutes of rest, I said that I felt better and we continued our normal walk, taking a few minutes to take the camera shots as planned. We had our brown bag lunches together on the campus and then went back to our desks for our busy afternoon schedules.

Later that day, one of my visitors said to me, "Chet, are you feeling well?" I replied, "Yes," as we generally do, but then told him about the chest pain I had experienced earlier. He, too, had been a heart patient and urged me to call my doctor. I finally did, minimizing any urgency because I wasn't experiencing much discomfort by the time I telephoned the doctor. He suggested I meet him in his office for an examination.

After studying my chest X ray and electrocardiogram, the doctor urged me to go to the hospital for an angiogram. This involves injecting a dye into the bloodstream and then taking moving X rays of the coronary arteries that can show exactly where the arteries are narrowed or blocked. I was sedated but conscious during the procedure and recall the cardiologist saying the arteries were severely blocked. The doctors then tried the angioplasty procedure, in which a small balloon is inflated in the artery in an attempt to compact the plaque against the walls of the artery, thus enlarging the arterial vessel for the free flow of blood into the heart muscle. I was conscious during this procedure and heard the medical personnel discussing the fact that they couldn't keep the channel open. They informed me I needed open-heart surgery and the surgical team was ready. I signed a release, was placed on a gurney, and moved into the elevator that led to the operating room. On that brief trip, my wife came to my side and whispered her support and prayer. As they wheeled me into the operating room someone "welcomed" me and the anesthesiologist began the preparation for my surgery. He told me to start counting down from ten. I said "ten . . . nine" and then I said, "Lord, into your hands I commend myself." That's all I remember—that prayer.

Many hours and a triple bypass later, I was in a recovery area. It was very early in the morning. In one ear, I heard the voice of a nurse saying something about surgery being over and everything was all right. I didn't know what she was talking about. I hadn't been mentally prepared for any surgery. In the other ear I heard a familiar voice saying, "This is Robert Schuller." He said a prayer of gratitude and implored God to heal me and I knew that I was in the land of the living. Then I remembered that prayer of the night before: "Lord, into your hands I commend myself."

A few nights later, after I was discharged from the hospital, I was in bed asleep for the night when I was suddenly overcome with a piercing chest pain—worse than the first that had precipitated the open heart surgery. My wife called the doctor, and in minutes, the paramedics, firemen, and ambulance attendants were taking me to the hospital for another emergency. This turned out to be a blood clot that had developed in my chest. That night, I said the same prayer, "Lord, into your hands I commend myself."

After several days of healing and convalescence, I returned home and began the regimented process of getting well. I attribute my recovery to a wise physician, skilled surgeons and attendants in the operating room, well-trained and caring nurses, encouraging therapists, therapeutic drugs, the support of family and friends, and prayer. All of the healing agents working together, for me, was the formula for success.

Prayer is a mighty force in that formula. It brings all the healing instruments together. It works! The key to prayer is faith; and the keys to faith are belief and trust. Trust is put into motion by commitment. To commit means to put oneself into the care of another. In prayer we are handing over ourselves—body, mind, and spirit—to God.

Life Changes and Prayer

Life offers many challenges, the ultimate being death itself. We are sometimes called upon to face pain, suffering, loss, and grief that may seem impossible to handle. Prayer gives us hope and keeps us moving. Here is a formula you may use to help overcome. When confronted with a trial of any kind:

1. Face it
2. Lift it
3. Commit it
4. Release it

Let's look at each of these in more detail:

Face it. One thing that adds enormous pressure to an already tense situation is our inability to face realistically what may be happening to us. We may be:

Fearful of the outcome
Unwilling to believe the facts
Embarrassed by the conditions
Protective of ourselves or others

Denying or avoiding a problem that requires action on our part is never helpful. Research has shown that people who do this regularly end up not coping as well. Studies of both college students and sick older adults demonstrate that those who approach their problems by avoidance and denial experience less well-being overall, compared to those who face their problems.[2]

Lift *it.* After facing up to the real facts of what is happening in your life or someone else's, or in the conditions around you, and having done everything you know or can do with the help of others, you must then lift these facts above yourself to God in prayer. At that point you make a full and complete disclosure of your needs. It is helpful to name them one by one. God does not need this recitation, but doing so strengthens us. We admit to ourselves that we cannot do it alone and we ask God for help.

Commit it. Having faced it and lifted it to God, we commit it. We take it out of our hands and hand it over to God. The solution to the problem will be through us from God's divine will for our lives. This commitment should be without any reserves. It is handed over in faith that God will handle it.

Release it. Having faced it, lifted it, and committed it, we must release it. We may not be able to forget it but we should release it and no longer worry about it.

A recent study of 73,424 people who were followed over eight years found that women who worried a lot (experienced high stress) were over twice as likely to experience a stroke, over twice as likely to experience coronary artery disease, and 64 percent more likely to die from heart disease. Men who worried a lot were 74 percent more likely to experience a heart attack than men who were less stressed.[3] Worry is bad for your health.

As the old gospel song suggested, you should "take your burden to the Lord and leave it there." Don't disturb this formula for healing by asking, "When, where, why, or how?" Remind yourself and the Lord that you are just *leaving it there.*

8

THE MIND AND PRAYER

*T*he whole person is involved in prayer: body, mind, and spirit. While praying, our minds should be focused on God, to whom we are speaking, and the subject matter we are discussing with him. This would be true for any good earthly conversation, and therefore is certainly not less important when talking with God. In prayer our words of praise, devotion, petition, and commitment should be deliberately expressed. It isn't that God needs to be clear but we need our minds to be clear to hear what God is saying back to us. Our heads as well as our hearts are active in prayer.

Prayer is more than a spoken catharsis of our fears and needs at times of crisis or a vain repetition of words. Prayer is thoughtful expression and thoughtful listening. Our minds should be fully engaged when we are praying. We call this experience *contemplation*. This term comes from the word *con* meaning "with" or "together" and the word *templum* meaning "a place of dedication to God." From this we get the word *temple* or *holy place*. This is God's habitat. In prayer we are literally at "God's place." Our minds ought to be functioning at peak performance. We should be thinking about God, our host. We should be striving to create mental images of God as sovereign, to whom we offer our adoration. We should acknowledge God as our provider, and name our blessings before him "one by one" in offering our prayer of gratitude and thanksgiving. Our minds ought to be engaged on the real needs of others, not merely naming their names, as we offer our prayers of intercession. Our minds should acknowledge our honest surrender and dedication to the Lord, the *kurios*—our ruler—as we offer our prayers of consecration. In other words, our minds should be actively involved in what we are praying about and to whom we are praying. Prayer is more than words for words' sake or form for form's sake.

The Brain and Prayer

Religious experiences and activities, such as prayer, involve our brains. Establishing visits with God has to do with the mental phenomenon called *habit*. When we pray, how we pray, and where we pray all must become a matter of habit. How is the brain involved in establishing a habit? Although there is not a lot of research in this area, neuropsychologists think that the establishment of repetitive patterns of activity occurs in the frontal regions of the brain (the part located under the forehead). In addition to mediating the habit of praying, different parts of the brain also become activated when we pray.

Scientists have attempted to measure the part of the brain that is active in prayer. This research is in its very earliest stages, and the radiological techniques that we have to measure such a complex phenomenon as prayer in the brain (electroencephalogram [EEG], positron emission tomography [PET], and single photon emission computed tomography [SPECT]), are still quite primitive. Quantitative MRI-PET imagery and functional MRI (fMRI) promise in the future to provide still further resolution and quantification of brain functioning during spiritual experiences. Almost all of this research, however, has examined Eastern meditation (transcendental or mindfulness meditation), not praying in a conversational manner to God. However, the following is what we know or at least think we know from what scientists have discovered.

The May 7, 2001, issue of *Newsweek* featured an article titled "God and the Brain: How We're Wired for Spirituality." This article discussed which parts of the brain become active and which parts quiet down during Buddhist meditation (the practice of sitting quietly and repeating a sound or phrase over and over again, dispelling all other thoughts from the mind). "Activity in the amygdala, which monitors the environment for threats and registers fear, must be damped. Parietal lobe circuits, which orient you in space and mark the sharp distinction between self and world, must go quiet. Frontal- and temporal-lobe circuits, which mark time and generate self-awareness, must disengage."[1] In this way, a Buddhist goes into a deeply relaxed state, where he becomes "at one" with the universe. Several scientists have written about the radiological changes in the brain that occur during meditation.[2]

This, however, is not the same kind of prayer that we are discussing. Is the person meditating in this way having a conversation with Someone who is separate from himself, a person with feelings and emotions who can be known and has a will and a purpose for humans that he wishes to communicate to them? Not really.

Nevertheless, the *Newsweek* article also talks about changes in the brain of a Franciscan nun, detected using SPECT-scanning, as she began to go into deep prayer. "During her most intensely religious moments," the article reports, "when she felt a palpable sense of God's presence and an absorption of her self into his being, her brain displayed changes like those in the Tibetan Buddhist meditators."

Be aware, however, that this is a single case in a single study, and the findings have not been replicated by different research scientists, as must occur before the result can be considered reliable. Furthermore, the experience of "union" with the external world—the universe, a beautiful flower, a sunset, or a night sky—does not necessarily imply that the person is communicating or having conversation with God. It may also occur at that time (as with the Franciscan nun), but such brain changes are not unique to spiritual experiences. Similar changes occur during a particularly intense emotional state—including, perhaps, the disorganization and disorientation that occurs with schizophrenia or other psychotic disorders, the experience that one has on LSD, cocaine, or heroin, or the strange states induced by temporal-lobe epilepsy.

Conversational prayer is something totally different. And there is almost no research on conversational prayer with God and brain activity. To our knowledge, there is only one such study in the scientific literature.[3] Researchers recorded the EEGs of six adult Church of God members both at rest and during prayer. All subjects were known to have a devout religious life. These investigators wanted to see if changes in the brain could be induced like those found with Transcendental Meditation. Each subject prayed during laboratory sessions in his or her own usual way, consisting of prayers of intercession, adoration or praise, confession, guidance, thanksgiving, and receiving from God. Brainwave speed before, during, and after prayer was recorded. Brainwave speed, however, was not significantly different between rest and prayer activity at any time during this experiment. PET, SPECT, and other radiological procedures have not yet been employed to study this kind of prayer.

Consequently, we really don't know what part of the brain is activated when we have a conversation with God. Our guess is that it is probably similar to the changes that are seen in the brain when a person is having a conversation with a friend or family member—someone who is loved and trusted. This could easily be studied, just as meditation has, using the radiological techniques described above, and we hope that someday it will be.

Another possibility has not received much attention, and that is the notion that we use the left side of our brains to communicate to God and the right side of our brains to receive from God. The left hemisphere of the brain is known to be more analytical, logical, and reasoning. It is also where the speech recognition and initiation areas of the brain are located. A stroke in this part of the brain will make it difficult for a person to speak. The right hemisphere of the brain has more to do with pattern recognition, artistic abilities, intuition, and the ability to sense other people's feelings. Thus, we may use different parts of our brain as we converse with God. While this may be interesting and reasonable, it has not been subject to scientific study. In practice, it doesn't really matter to us what parts of our brains are involved in praying to God, since it all occurs very naturally and normally. Indeed, it may be the prayers of children, who know nothing at all about "how" prayer works, that are the most powerful because of their sincerity and unquestioning faith.

Contemplation and Prayer

Conversational prayer is not only about what we do, but also about what God does. God directs us through contemplation. Contemplation includes the conscious and the subconscious mind activities. A person has a deep problem to face. He seems unable to find the answer or direction for solving his problem. Before going to sleep, he prays about it. While praying he contemplates the possible answers known to him. He finally goes to sleep. The next morning, upon awakening, he realizes the solution to his problem. Even though his conscious mind was not active while sleeping, his subconscious mind remained on duty. As the answer came to the subconscious mind, it was transferred to the conscious mind for definitive action.

Contemplation is the phase of prayer that allows our petitions to settle down below the conscious level into that great storage area of the subconscious. We know that what entered our minds in early life has a profound and lasting influence throughout our entire lives. The field of analytical psychiatry has done much to demonstrate the importance of facing these mental roadblocks and overcoming them. But subconscious reception does not end at any time in our lives. We are constantly putting thoughts, ideas, and concepts into our subconscious mind. At this level it may be that God can more easily communicate to us his wisdom for answering our problems and his will for our lives. While God also speaks directly into our conscious minds, there is a greater chance that the many distractions of the world can crowd out his messages to us. Prayer is a way to open up this great reservoir to receive input from God for solutions to our needs and our problems.

Contemplation also includes imagination. How do we imagine ourselves to be? Someone has said, "We are what we think we are." While that is not totally true, allowing our minds to dwell on the positive instead of negative images of ourselves can affect what we "bring into God's temple." We do control our attitudes and responses. Our part in praying is to try to put out of our minds doubts, fears, and pessimistic thoughts.

Remember:

> If we believe we are beaten,
> Our thoughts may block our victory.
> If we are afraid to believe,
> We may not understand the answer.
> If we want to achieve but do nothing,
> Our lethargy may block our accomplishments.
> If we think we are going to lose,
> We may set in motion our defeat.
> But with God's help we can win,
> Whatever our struggles may be.
> Our attitude, our faith, and our determination
> Will help ignite the spark of grace.
> For us to understand and do whatever
> God wills for our lives.

This optimistic poem brings to our attention the importance of our own positive thoughts and imagination as we enter our contemplation with God. Negative thoughts can block the dialogue process between us and God.

There was a woman who said that she prayed often, yet she was constantly distressed. If you were to ask her how she was feeling, she would always go into a long and weepy discourse on how unfortunate she was. She was always holding a "pity party" for herself. No one else wanted to attend. She would end her negative and dreary recital with, "Oh well, it's all in the Lord's hands." How did it get there? Her attitude showed that she had not left her problems in God's hands, but rather kept a firm grasp of them on her own. Her attitude blocked her prayers up front. Does God hear us regardless of our attitude? Probably so, but if we have blocked out our minds with negative and hateful thoughts, how can we expect to discern God's positive will for us? We need a prayer attitude that affirms, not an attitude that denies.

Contemplation also requires waiting and quietness. As the psalmist wrote: "Rest in the LORD, and wait patiently for Him" (Ps. 37:7). This means listening quietly and allowing our thoughts to rest, so that God can communicate his love and wisdom to us. "Be still [quiet and peaceful], and know that I am God (Ps. 46:10). This is often a difficult thing to do.

A woman, who had been asking people to pray for her because of her dysfunctional family life, was asked how things were going. She replied, "I don't know. I've been too busy to listen to the Lord."

To rest in the Lord and wait patiently on him means that we open up our minds to receive what God has to give. This is the contemplative part of prayer. Waiting for God's answer to our prayers becomes easier and more natural the longer and more regularly we pray.

The Mind of Christ and Prayer

Since our minds are so actively involved in prayer, we should do all we can to manage our thoughts so that we can receive from God. In addition to our own thought-management efforts, we should strive to make the mind of Jesus our model. In writing to the Christians at Philippi, Paul said, "Let this mind be in you which was also in Christ Jesus" (Phil. 2:5). He went on to say that the mind of Jesus, who is to be our model, evidences itself in:

- Humbleness
- Servanthood

- Willingness to suffer for others
- Love of others
- Obedience to God

These qualities and attributes should be influencing our minds as we enter our visits with God. Addressing the church at Rome, Paul emphasized that this same mind of Christ should be our model:

- Love without hypocrisy
- Abhor evil
- Cling to the good
- Be kindly and affectionate to one another
- Don't be lazy and let others do all the work
- Try to carry your own burdens
- Be enthusiastic
- Serve the Lord
- Be joyful
- Have hope
- Be patient
- Pray regularly
- Concern yourselves with others' needs
- Give to others
- Be friendly
- Don't hold a grudge
- Bless your enemies
- Rejoice when others are happy
- Mourn with those who mourn
- Don't plan revenge

Paul said to these Christians at Rome that these qualities reflect the mind of Christ (Rom. 12:9–15). He then exhorted, "Be of the same mind toward one another" (Rom. 12:16), adding that these qualities of mind would produce humility, fairness, justice, goodness, and peace. This is why it is so important to have the mind of Christ as the model for our minds during prayer.

Developing this mind of Jesus during our times of prayer and between our times of prayer is not a burden, an impossible dream, or a hopeless task. When we are new creatures in Christ, we avail ourselves of these qualities of mind.

We know that the brain is complex and has many functions. Someone has suggested our regular mundane thoughts based on logic and rationalization could be visualized as a horizontal line. On the other hand, dreams, intuitions, and spiritual thoughts could be visualized as being vertical. These two lines converge to form a cross. Through this imagery we should see Jesus Christ as the master of our minds. In this context we enter prayer.

9

SERENITY AND PRAYER

*T*he results of our visits with God are real and measurable. We leave those prayer times changed, blessed, and with purpose. We enter into that conversation with God just as we are. No pretense is needed; in fact, no pretense is possible. We know that our "ticket to get in" is through the grace and love of God.

Tension and Prayer

Sometimes, we enter God's presence in a hurried moment and with an urgent request. These prayers are vital and important. But that is not all there is to prayer. We should seek and develop conversation with God on a regular basis. One of the primary requirements for any successful conversation is that both parties be calm and receptive. Shouldn't this same principle apply for our visits with God in prayer? God, by his very nature, is not tense and preoccupied. But many times we are. Our tension makes it difficult for us to hear that still, small voice. Tension is a common problem for many of us. The word *tension* comes from the word *torsio* which means "to tighten." We describe ourselves when we are tense as being "uptight." The opposite of tension is relaxation, which means to be loose again.

Tension may lead to serious health problems as well. Medical research has documented an alarmingly high number of illnesses and deaths precipitated by tension in daily life. The difficulty we have in being able to relax and be quiet may be a significant factor in premature death. Tensions in our contemporary society are creating high tempers, high blood pressure, and high anxiety. The slang words a generation uses often reflect what it values. Some of the buzz words of our day—*Wow! Tight! Rad! Awesome! Super! Jam!*—suggest that today's generation is driven by things that are fast, big, and overt. Our slang words place little emphasis on quietness, waiting, and humility.

Living in the fast lane all the time may be one reason why we're uptight. A "split second" has been defined as that interval of time between the changing of the traffic signal light from red to green and the honking of the car immediately behind. This uptightness can cause us serious trouble. We must learn to let go.

As noted above, tension can be responsible for a plethora of social and health problems. Tension also causes havoc in human relationships, as we tend to be more impatient, irritable, and easily angered and less flexible, tolerant, understanding, and forgiving. A high-tension lifestyle can contribute to divorce, alcoholism, drug use, risky sexual behaviors, and auto accidents. The physical body can also be directly affected by chronic tension. The systems that are most affected are the cardiovascular and the immune systems. Tension elevates levels of adrenaline in the blood, which constricts blood vessels and raises blood pressure, increases the oxygen demand of the heart (increasing the likelihood of heart attack), and induces heart muscle irritability, causing cardiac arrhythmias. Tension also suppresses immune functioning, increasing susceptibility to infection, development and spread of cancer, and slow wound healing.

Simply put, in this wonderful instrument we call our body, we have a communications control system, called the autonomic nervous system. It controls the function of the glands, the smooth muscle tissues, and the heart. If we are uptight, the nervous system notifies the vital organs and glands, which immediately go into action. For example, the adrenal glands secrete very little adrenaline during ordinary activities. However, under the influence of tension, pain, fear, or rage these glands secrete large amounts. The adrenaline stimulates the heart and enables it to meet the needs of the physical emergency. This special boost is a positive and vital factor for these extraordinary occasions. That's the good news! Yet if we are living under tension much of the time, an abnormal amount of adrenaline is secreted over a long period. This can lead to the serious complications described above. This tension may even affect our prayer life. That's the bad news!

Someone has compared prayer to a telephone call with a dear friend. In order to have a successful and meaningful conversation, the line must be clear. If there seems to be static on the line when we are talking to God in prayer, the problem is usually on our end of the line. Could it be that our tension may act as interference hampering reception? Since humans are a trinity of body, mind, and spirit, what can we do to clear the static?

Relaxation and Prayer

First of all, relax the body. Today we are very body conscious. We spend a great deal of time and money firming up and toning our bodies. We are learning that physical activity and exercise are not only good for our cardiovascular health but that they also relieve tension. A simple exercise that will relax the muscles in the arms, legs, and neck will help in relieving tension. Sitting loosely with the palms of the hands turned up in an attitude of receptivity will turn your attention away from anxious thoughts to being "on purpose" for a visit with God. Simple breathing exercises and focusing on our breathing will quiet us and make us more receptive.

After the tension in the body is released, relax the mind. We need to let go of mental worries and center our thoughts on God. This is sometimes facilitated by using the imagination. Substitute an anxious thought with a thought of a quiet place. This may be a real place once visited or a place made up in the imagination. For example, the imaginer may think about a quiet green meadow, a calm lake, a gently swaying tree, or the splash of seawater back and forth against the silent rocks of a cove. Or he may imagine himself in the quietness of a chapel with light filtering in through stained glass windows. Imagination and mental recall can create a quietness and stillness that releases our tension.

Within this serene mental setting, the person in prayer should deliberately turn his thoughts away from malice and hate. Any desire of retaliation and anger, which will cause tension and block the spiritual connection to God, should be released.

Instead, we should focus our attention on kind thoughts and forgiving thoughts about those who have set out to harm us. This was a formula that Jesus suggested: "But I say to you, love your enemies, bless those who curse you, do good to those who hate you, and pray for those who spitefully use you and persecute you" (Matt. 5:44). Such thoughts will help release your tension and create greater receptivity in prayer. As we enter into this visit with God, we should deliberately turn our thoughts from loathing to loving. This attitude change will prepare our minds for entrance into the presence of the Almighty.

Finally, we should relax the spirit by turning ourselves over to God. We should experience God as sovereign, majestic, eternal, holy, and our most trusted friend. In our imagination we see ourselves entering God's presence. It may be helpful to recite familiar passages of Scripture that describe the peace that comes through God's presence. "Come to Me, all you who labor and are heavy laden, and I will give you rest" (Matt. 11:28) or "You will keep him in perfect peace, whose mind is stayed on You" (Isa. 26:3). Thinking thoughts about God will release your tension. Quietly, think about God as Creator, Provider, Savior, and Companion. Quietly say these words to yourself and think about what each word means to you. These thoughts will move you from your anxious world to his tranquil presence.

Another tension easer is to think about or recite a favorite hymn, such as the beautiful one by Henry F. Lyte:

> Abide with me: fast falls the eventide;
> The darkness deepens; Lord, with me abide:
> When other helpers fail, and comforts flee,
> Help of the helpless, O abide with me!

Many hymns, praise songs, and spiritual choruses can put your spirit into an appropriate posture for your visit with God.

Reciting a poem may also prepare you. The lines from Tennyson's "The Passing of Arthur," from *Idylls of the King* might be helpful:

> . . . More things are wrought by prayer
> than this world dreams of.
> Wherefore, let Thy voice
> rise like a fountain for me night and day.

These verses, and others you may recall, will impress upon your consciousness the very presence of God and help put you in a quiet, relaxed, and receptive mood.

We are describing a way of getting ourselves prepared for this divine/human encounter. We are *not* saying that prayer is possible because of things we do. Prayer is driven by grace. We are responsible, however, for creating a receptive spiritual environment. It follows that our part of the conversation with God will be enhanced if we are more tension free. Pushing into the presence of God with a barrage of loud, fast words and having our minds preoccupied with stress and tension may not make prayer as meaningful to us as it ought to be.

Another helpful way to relieve tension during this great visit is to have a quiet place, away from the traffic of the day, where we can retreat into God's presence. Find a spot that you identify with God. Of course, God is not limited to your spot, but it becomes a place naturally associated with your spiritual visit. We can pray anywhere at anytime, but, here we are considering developing a habit of conversation with God. And that needs a regular place to meet him.

Several additional "tension relievers" may also be helpful in creating an atmosphere of peace and receptiveness:

- Visual aids such as a spiritual painting suggesting a quiet time
- An open Bible
- A lighted candle
- A symbolic cross
- Meditative music

These are all helpful means for reducing stress, getting us focused, and otherwise preparing us for our visit with God. Sometimes, before beginning our prayer, it may enhance our receptivity to stop and take a long look out the window, if such a view is possible. See the sweeping view of God's handiwork in nature. Look for evidence of God's creativity and affirm that God is at work there too. If you don't have such a view, then imagine. In your imagination do as the psalmist suggested:

> I will lift my eyes to the hills—
> From whence comes my help?
> My help comes from the LORD,
> Who made heaven and earth.
>
> Psalm 121:1

Reassuring ourselves, in prayer, that we really are in the very presence of God is necessary. Say or sing to yourself the words of the familiar hymn written by Maltbie D. Babcock in 1901:

> This is my Father's world,
> And to my list'ning ears,
> All nature sings, and round me rings
> The music of the spheres.

This is my Father's world,
I rest me in the thought
Of rocks and trees, of skies and seas;
His hand the wonders wrought.

This is my Father's world,
The birds their carols raise;
The morning light, the lily white
Declare their Maker's praise.
This is my Father's world,
He shines in all that's fair;
In the rustling grass I hear Him pass,
He speaks to me ev'rywhere.

This is my Father's world,
Oh, let me ne'er forget
That though the wrong seems oft so strong,
God is the Ruler yet.
This is my Father's world,
The battle is not done;
Jesus who died shall be satisfied,
And earth and heaven be one.

These confirmations of the sovereignty and compassion of God prepare us further for our healing visits with him.

Finally, we should make good use of silence. In this conversation we must allow time for the Spirit of God to speak to our spirits. These periods of quietness are like the white space on this printed page; it makes the type stand out more clearly. Those moments of quiet waiting will impress upon our minds the will and purpose of God in our lives. The answers will come. We can count on it!

In Practice

Someone once suggested that the most meaningful prayer experience is like floating in the water. The more relaxed we are, the easier and longer we stay afloat. We should strive to be as serene as possible for this most important visit.

J. B. was a typical man on the move. He had an extroverted personality. He was driven by the urge to succeed in everything he did, and wanted to dominate his situation. He would say, "I won't surrender to anyone or anything." Outwardly, he appeared to be winning. Ethically and morally, he sometimes seemed to cut a fine line. But generally speaking he enjoyed a good reputation among his close family and friends. They would overlook his living on the edge and simply say, "Well, that's J. B."

J. B. was not happy with himself. He suffered from low self-esteem. He tried to compensate by making "show off" social moves and working constantly. Religion was not a meaningful part of his life. He occasionally went to church on Christmas and Easter because his wife, Susan, insisted he go with her and the boys. At weddings and funerals, he would sit in the pew, feel uncomfortable with the sacred surroundings, and let his mind wander. He tolerated Susan attending church with the kids and singing in the choir. He would rationalize this division in their marital union by saying, "Well, Susan is doing her thing."

At forty-nine years of age, at what J. B. liked to say was the "prime of his life," he had a heart attack. He was forced to think about his own mortality. J. B. began to attend church on Sundays, and found he enjoyed the pastor's sermons. In fact, he liked the pastor and invited him to play a round of golf with him at the country club. To his surprise, the pastor was a good golfer. They became friends. Through the pastor's invitation he began attending a seekers class on Wednesday evenings. Susan was thrilled to attend with him. For the first time in his life, J. B. listened to the story about the life, death, and resurrection of Jesus Christ. He was introduced to the Bible. His friend, the pastor, encouraged him to read the Book of Romans. During personal visits, Pastor Jim explained the plan of redemption and the hope J. B. had for a new life in Christ. In one of these private meetings, J. B. said his first real prayer and accepted Christ as the Lord of his life.

J. B. truly became a new person. He could relate to Paul's words to the Corinthians: "Therefore, if anyone is in Christ, he is a new creation; old things have passed away; behold all things are new" (2 Cor. 5:17). As Jesus had said to Nicodemus, "Unless one is born again, he cannot see the kingdom of God" (John 3:3). J. B. let everyone know that he had been born again. It showed in all his relationships. He joined the church and became involved in several of its mission programs. He was gung ho for his new life but he had moments of spiritual depression. He had trouble praying.

He discussed this with Pastor Jim, who observed that although J. B. was a new creature in Christ, he still had many of the personality traits of the old J. B. His pastor suggested that maybe he was bringing his "fast lane" approach and worried thoughts into his conversation with God. Pastor Jim suggested that J. B. use some simple tools for easing his tension as he prepared himself for prayer. But J. B. resisted these suggestions as sounding too "New Age" to him. Pastor Jim was surprised with this reaction, given J. B.'s nonreligious background. He explained to J. B. that these tension-easing techniques were not new. He recited passages from the Old and New Testaments to J. B. to support his suggestion. Consequently J. B. began to reserve special times for prayer. He was introduced to several good relaxation techniques to help him become more receptive in prayer. He stopped saying, "It seems God doesn't hear me," and instead was able to enter prayer in a more peaceful and serene manner, more patient and willing to wait on God.

For J. B., prayer has become one of the most positive forces he has ever experienced. His lifestyle has changed and his cardiovascular problems are under control.

Prayer really works. We are at our best when we make it a habit to have visits with God.

10

FOCUS AND FOLLOW-THROUGH IN PRAYER

W hatever gets your attention, gets you! That statement is a headline for our daily lives. So much hangs on what we are attentive to. *Attention, focus,* and *concentration* all mean about the same thing. *Concentration* comes from two words, *con*, meaning "with" or "together" from the Latin *cum*, and *centrum*, meaning "center." This definition paints a word picture of what is happening when we pay attention, get focused, or concentrate. We are bringing things to the very center of our thought system. This ordinary, everyday process may make all the difference in the world in our lives. In a split second, our total lives can change if we are not focused.

Barbara was a good person, a fine wife, and a good mother. She was respected at the middle school where she taught and was highly regarded for her work in the community and devotion to her church. Everything was going along fine in her well-ordered world. It was 4:30 P.M. on Wednesday afternoon. She had just finished her day at the school. She was on her way to the market to get a few things for dinner. Suddenly, her purse flipped over on the passenger seat next to her. Her attention was diverted for a split second. As she reached over to pick up something to put back in the open purse, in that instant, her arm accidentally turned the steering wheel into another car carrying four people. Two of the four passengers in the other car were killed. Barbara received some injuries, but her life was never the same. That split second made the difference.

Bob was a hard worker. He had been with the same organization for seven years and had risen to a position in middle management. He was well liked and his bosses had their eyes on Bob for future leadership. On this particular Friday morning, he was seated at the conference table. A consultant was making a presentation on ideas for restructuring Bob's department. For some reason, Bob let his mind wander to the mountain house he and Virginia were planning to build. He was sketching out a floor plan for the cabin. Something was said that he should have heard. His distraction was only for a couple of minutes, but during that brief time a proposal was presented that he didn't catch. Following the meeting, his boss, who was presiding at the meeting, asked him what he thought of the presentation and particularly the consultants' suggestion that they merge two departments. Bob drew a blank. He stuttered and tried to "punt" his way out, but it didn't work. The boss recognized that Bob was not paying attention; this cost him the promotion the company was considering for him. Those brief moments of mental wandering had an enormous effect on Bob and his family.

Cathy was a good student. Her grades meant a lot to her. She was looking forward to moving ahead into a graduate program. A good grade in this class would be important in her academic plans. The professor was detailing a point on the philosophical impact of a prominent author's new concept of man and the cosmos. She had no idea that the subject would be a central theme in the upcoming final exam. She missed what the professor was saying completely. She didn't even make any reference in her notebook. In fact she was thinking about her social life and was writing down the names of the guys she found most interesting. That whole section on man and the cosmos just went by her. It cost her dearly in exam points. She thought it wasn't fair, but the fact remained that Cathy wasn't focused when she should have been.

Frank and Eleanor had been married for ten years. They somehow made it that long, but when they finally decided to end their marriage, they both agreed that neither of them had really listened to the other. Frank did his thing and Eleanor did her thing. They went to social activities together, shopped together, and occasionally went to church together. Eleanor's mother said their problem was that they didn't have children. It turned out to be a good thing that they were childless, because the children would have faced a broken home. The real problem for Frank and Eleanor was that they never communicated because they never focused their full attention on one another.

These stories of real life all teach us the same lesson.

- Barbara's open purse distracted her attention for that tragic split second, which ended in the death of two innocent people.
- Bob's momentary lack of concentration caused him to lose a job promotion.
- Cathy's daydreaming derailed her academic plans.
- Frank and Eleanor's lack of attention to each other caused them to end their relationship.

All of these stories highlight the truth that whatever has your focus and attention will determine the direction of your life.

An Associated Press article stated that nearly 30 percent of automobile crashes happen because of the drivers' inattention at the wheel. Formerly the most common distractions were eating, smoking, children, pets, reading, and personal hygiene. Now these distractions run well behind cell phones, radio-CD systems, and even television and DVD movies. How can we drive a car, weighing tons, at high speeds, while diverting our attention to other activities? Yet we do it. It results in injuries and deaths for millions.

The part of the brain called the reticular activating system (RAS) is located deep within the primitive brain stem that we humans share with almost all other animal forms. The RAS enables us to focus our attention on a single activity while filtering out other stimuli from inside and outside that might distract us from the task at hand. Certain mental disorders are associated with damage to the RAS, including conditions such as attention deficit hyperactivity disorder (ADHD). The RAS is the key to "turning on your brain" and seems to be the center of motivation. This complex network of neurons enables us to concentrate. Disruption of this system can even lead to loss of consciousness and coma. Overactivation of this system can lead to hyperactivity, hypervigilance, and anxiety—symptoms of ADHD.

At least two million children suffer from ADHD (3 to 10 percent of school-age children), and many of these continue to have problems with attention in adulthood. Although hyperactivity declines with age, problems with attention tend to persist. Other psychiatric conditions, learning disabilities, and social difficulties are commonly associated with difficulties concentrating and paying attention. Although around 5 percent of adults have the brain disorder ADHD that could explain our inattention, the remaining 95 percent of us don't have that excuse. We simply have not developed the habit of focused concentration, since this requires a lot of motivation and retraining of our brains.

Attention and Prayer

Being able to focus is critical for success and accomplishment, which require sustained attention in moving toward a goal. If we are constantly distracted, we get off on rabbit trails and never reach our intended destination. Developing the ability to focus and concentrate is essential for accomplishing any task successfully, including prayer.

As illustrated in the stories above, lack of concentration can be harmful. We have all learned the importance of majoring on one thing at a time if we hope to progress in our academic learning. The teacher recognizes this as a primary factor in the educational experience. If a student is unable to concentrate upon the subject being presented, and allows his mind to wander, it becomes almost impossible to receive information on the subject being presented.

This vital subject of focus is fundamental to every form of human behavior. Sports, education, entertainment, and work all require focus for success. For example, golf requires intense concentration. One lapse of mental attention may be disastrous as one commits an error in the club swing. As we watch the professionals on television play their magnificent golf rounds, we see them totally focused on the one shot they are playing at that moment. Even the camera must stay focused. Many golfers have had the experience of playing a rather good game and then falling into conversation. As a result, the game goes to pieces. Later, as the golfer looks back over the score card, he can recall the conversation that caused the problem and made a good game go bad.

When I (Chet) was pastor of the Village Church in Rancho Santa Fe, California, our congregation was made up of many people who were world famous in their chosen fields. These champions all told similar stories about the key to their success.

Charles "Pete" Conrad Jr. was an astronaut. I remember the day he was selected to be a part of this elite group. We were having a dinner meeting for the young married couples at the church. The Conrads were regular attendees. That day, Pete, an outstanding test pilot, was told he was selected to be a part of the Gemini space project. He was to be the pilot of Gemini 5 and 11. Later he would walk on the moon. Earlier that particular day he shared this important information with me, his pastor, and instructed me not to share it with anybody until the public announcement the next day. That evening, after we finished dinner, the young men went outside for fresh air while their wives packed the potluck plates and bowls. It was full moon that night. I couldn't resist asking Pete if he thought there would be a real human someday on the moon. He smiled and replied, "Yes, sometime."

After his "moon shot," I asked him what was the most important part of being an astronaut. He replied instantly, "Staying focused on what you are doing." He went on to explain that the training was excellent, and he had good knowledge of what was happening. He said that "mission control" had things well organized for the mission but his main job was to stay focused on every detail of his role in the mission. He couldn't be distracted, whether he was on a Gemini or an Apollo moon mission. Concentration was the key in his role in space exploration.

Amelita Galli-Curci was an opera singer. Many say she may have been the leading soprano of all time. *Encyclopædia Britannica* says that her voice was "exceptionally fluent, warm, and smooth." She could hold the Metropolitan audience in the "palms of her hands" during the many years of performing there. Her repertoire included twenty-eight operatic roles. I visited her weekly and prayed with her. These were her later years of life, and she reflected often about her amazing career. I felt honored talking to someone who had risen to the very top of her profession. One day, I asked her why she had become so successful. She attributed it to three things:

1. Natural gifts. Things only God had given her. She studied piano and composition at Milan Royal Conservatory, but as a singer she was self-taught.
2. Practice and hard work. She said that by consistent trial she learned just how to "place the tone" for the best production.
3. Concentration. She said that this was probably the thing that made her stand out among the others. She said she learned very early how to "put on the blinders." When performing she couldn't let her mind wander to "anything that would distract her from the score, tone placement, and pleasing the audience." The ability to focus made the difference in her success.

Robert Young was an actor. His two television shows, *Father Knows Best* and *Marcus Welby, M.D.*, had the highest TV viewer ratings of programs during their times. His acting gifts were outstanding, and he worked hard to become the best in his profession. We were good friends. He participated, on occasion, in our worship service. We played golf together and spent time talking about the guiding principles for living. I asked him what was the most important factor in his success. He replied, "Staying focused on the script, the character I'm playing, and getting my message across."

What about prayer and concentration? We know the importance of focusing our attention upon the person with whom we are conversing. This is a chief ingredient for meaningful conversation. Since prayer is conversation with God, concentration becomes a major factor. If we are merely saying words, but paying little attention to the God with whom we are speaking, how do we expect to have a dialogue? Prayer without focusing and listening is really a monologue. If God were not concentrating on us, how could we receive direction? It is mutual attention, a true rapport, that gives life and meaning to prayer.

Attention, focus, and concentration—three words that mean about the same thing—are vital for living and paramount in praying. Thankfully, they are largely under our control. However, we must deliberately make an effort to stay focused. Jesus put it this way: "When you pray, go into your room, and shut the door" (Matt. 6:6). That's it! Shut the door on anything and any thought that would intrude and interrupt. Contemplate. Move into the temple. Center your thoughts there.

Focusing our attention on God makes prayer work. Prayer has its own dominant purpose. It is like the major C chord in all our clamoring discords. When we center our minds on prayer, then prayer in turn centers us. Jesus prayed most of the night about his future death and finally surrendered to his Father by saying, "Not as I will, but as You will" (Matt. 26:39). To be able to become saturated with this desire to focus on God should be the goal of every human being who has been created in the very image of God (Gen. 1:26). Paul, in his letter to the Philip-

pians said, "For to me, to live is Christ" (Phil. 1:21). That is a
total commitment. In order to get to that point he said, "One
thing I do" (Phil. 3:13). Becoming so centered that we focus on
"one thing" requires grace and help from God. That is available
constantly. Prayer enables that grace. It takes the same "one
thing I do" attitude on our part to get us into the prayer mode
and keep us there.

The Five Senses and Prayer

Attention, by its very nature, is selective. We can be distracted by many factors. For example, the five senses constantly
compete for our attention: Hearing, touching, seeing, smelling,
and tasting can all interrupt our concentration. Sounds draw
our attention to events around us. Physical sensations such
as hot or cold cause discomfort that distracts us from our task
at hand. Sights and smells capture our focus and disrupt our
concentration. Tastes activate either the pleasure or the disgust
centers of the brain and can scream for our attention. In con-
trast, each of these five senses can also help us to concentrate
during prayer.

We should consider each of these senses when creating our
environment for an effective visit with God. It will be helpful
to go to our "quiet place" whenever we can, away from the
confusion and clamor around us. The very effort of going to
such a spot begins the focusing process.

Use your own natural senses to get your attention focused:

Hearing. Passages from the Bible, other prayers, and meditative works, when read aloud to oneself or listened to on tape or
CD, will focus your attention. Quiet music, especially familiar
music with meaningful words, will move your attention from
external happenings and focus your thoughts on what you are
doing in prayer. Let your own auditory system work for you.

Seeing. What your eyes see has an enormous influence on
your focus and attention. Look at the time-honored symbols
of the cross, the Bible, a lighted candle, a picture, a sculpture

piece, or words that call your attention to prayer. One person has a tapestry hanging in his "praying place" that reads, "Life is fragile; handle with prayer!" This visual gets him focused. Make your sense of sight work for you in prayer.

Touching. Many religious people use this sense of touch for focusing in prayer. Some religious traditions use prayer beads as a means of focus. One woman who wouldn't think of using "prayer beads" had a favorite well-worn handkerchief that had belonged to her praying mother, which she treasured. She held it during her times of private devotion. She wasn't praying to the handkerchief, but she had discovered that this small precious piece of cloth helped her to concentrate on the fact that she was praying. The sense of touch may help you focus in prayer.

Smelling. Many people use the sense of smell to capture their attention. For example, the very aroma of the incense says to the worshiper that he or she is in God's presence. Or an aroma of a lighted candle may remind us that our prayers are a sweet-smelling aroma to God. We use smell all the time in our daily activities to attract attention. What good real estate salesperson hasn't learned the value of the aroma of an apple pie when showing a house for sale to an interested prospect? Everyone knows how the smell of a hanging wreath helps focus attention on Christmas. Every romantic man or woman knows the value of a delightful cologne or perfume. In prayer, the sense of smell may help to concentrate your focus as well.

Tasting. Some religious people use the taste of "holy" foods to help them focus on the object of their worship or the theme of their prayers. This is common to the ceremonies of many religious traditions. Certain meals at certain times in the religious calendar year hold important meaning to some people and bring their memories back to holy things. They are using the sense of taste to help them focus.

None of these suggestions for the senses are in themselves the meaning of prayer. Care must be taken that any of these holy uses of the senses do not become routine or a substitute for real spiritual substance. They should be considered for what they really are: strategies for focusing our attention upon God and the content of our prayers.

Prayer Techniques

The very best way to understand prayer is to pray. The very best way to learn how to pray is to practice it. The technique of prayer and the uses of aids in praying are secondary to the praying experience itself. Many faithful and sincere people have prayed for years without using any technique or sensory device. Whatever strategy is used, we must always remember the purpose: to keep our attention on God as we visit with him.

What about *posture* during prayer? Some people kneel, others sit, some stand, others lie down, still others might fall prostrate. Much has been said and practiced on the subject of posture and prayer. Some of the early churchmen recommended that the worshiping congregation should stand to say the Lord's Prayer and then advance one step to kneel and continue praying. Certainly, the position that is most natural and meaningful to use is the one you should employ. You have no responsibility to impose that on others, and they have no authority to impose their prayer posture on you.

Of course posture is related to health and other physical factors. When a person stands for a long period, the muscles become tenser and the body may fatigue. For the average person, this posture would not be preferable for long periods. Some people enjoy kneeling, if their physical body permits, because it represents to them a sign of reverence and humility. In that position they are focused on praying and that is helpful.

Others find a comfortable place to sit. They tolerate this position for a longer period. In any position, bowing the head tends to create an attitude of quietness. This prevents us from being distracted by other activities in our environment.

Closing the eyes cuts out visual distractions, yet there are "focus values" to keeping them open to see certain visual aids to center our thoughts. As a general rule, most people may find sitting with eyes open when focusing on symbols in the external

environment and then closed when reflecting and contemplat-
ing to be the best physical position in prayer, especially for the
beginner. The key is staying alert and focused, while at the same
time being in a position of rest and quiet.

To pray silently or audibly is another consideration. Some
find it easier to organize and focus their thoughts when praying
aloud. We hear what we are saying. The sounds of our words
will call attention to what we are doing and aid our concentration. When praying aloud, our prayers should be clear and
direct. We should speak as naturally as speaking to a friend. But
it is God we are speaking with, and we need not voice our words
audibly if it is uncomfortable or if the setting precludes it. (We
do not need to keep our family awake while we pray in a loud
voice.) Remember what Jesus said about going into the closet
and closing the door for prayer. Our silent thoughts speak just
as loudly as the words that come out of our mouths.

Whether your prayers are vocal or silent, they should carry
the same expectations and clarity. However we form and express
our prayers, we must remember that we are only one side of the
conversation. There should be moments of deliberate silence
where we are quietly waiting on God. This prayer rhythm that
moves back and forth between us and God brings wholeness
to the experience of prayer. We speak and then we listen for
his response.

"Prayer fatigue" may sometimes occur. This may be caused by
physical or emotional distress. If this is the case, the distressed
person should seek professional help. This fatigue may also be
due to the fact that one's prayer life is becoming too repetitious.
The complaint is sometimes heard, "I just seem to say the same
thing over and over again." One answer to that is to enlarge the
prayer agenda. Include the needs of others you know and the
problems affecting people you do not know. Another helpful
activity is to read the prayers of others. An anthology of prayers
from the Bible (you will find a list on page 159), a devotional
booklet, or a prayer calendar will help lift a person's prayer out
of sameness and add new enthusiasm for praying. Whatever
"prayer enlargers" you use, don't merely read the prayer. Study
it and listen to it. Project your personality, thoughts, and desires

into that written prayer. Make those written prayers your own prayers.

Some people find that writing down a prayer is helpful. This will add focus to what you are praying about. The written expression will deepen the impression. Many times, if you write down a prayer you will read it again. This helps to focus you on your petitions and adds to your level of commitment. Writing down your prayers may help increase their meaning, because you have created a written statement. Of course it is not necessary to write every prayer. Some may face a problem of sight or writing ability. This does not mean their prayer life is handicapped. For those who can, try it from time to time. It will help enlarge your prayer agenda, help keep you focused, and add a dimension of commitment to your prayers. (Beginning on page 167 we have included a thirty-day prayer diary for you to write some of your prayers.)

When is the best time to pray? Of course the answer is *anytime*. God is always there. A routine time for prayer is as beneficial to the soul as regular hours for sleep are to the body. As much as possible, set a certain time when you will meet with God. This will help enormously in keeping you focused.

One man was falling apart emotionally. His counselor suggested that he needed to develop some disciplines to improve his attention. He suggested that the next morning when he was shaving, the man do nothing but concentrate on his shaving. Focus on giving himself the best shave possible. He suggested he do this for the next ten days. This simple little procedure helped him get control of his scattering thoughts in other areas of his life. It is the "one thing I do" principle.

In prayer, if we develop consistent prayer times and if we "red letter" that event on the calendar of our daily lives, we will be on our way to a disciplined prayer life. Fit the prayer period into the most workable time slot in your schedule and try to keep it there.

For many people, early mornings are best. At this time of the day, the mind and body are usually refreshed. During sleep the subconscious mind has been at work sharpening your prayer requests from yesterday. The morning prayer also helps set the mood for the day and furnishes the one who prays with a spiritual glow and guide for the rest of the day. Morning prayer is like putting on the spiritual garment that will protect you from the challenges you may face that day. What strength will come if we open the windows of our soul every morning and gaze upon God! From that vision, we turn confident to meet the day. Morning prayers ought to stress adoration, surrender, petition, and intercession. This will consciously keep us in the awareness zone, where we will discipline our thoughts and actions in the light of our dedication to God. Then we can be alert to opportunities to seize the answers to our petitions and to help others in meeting their needs. The morning prayer sets all of this in motion.

The evening prayer ought to be reflective of the day. It will focus on the blessings God provided us during the day and confession of how we may have sinned in thought, word, or deed. We will reflect upon opportunities we may have missed and talk with God about wisdom, courage, and purpose.

In the evening prayer, we again offer our petitions for our needs and intercession for the needs of others. These thoughts enter our subconscious mind and prayer continues while we sleep. During evening prayers we may hear that still, small voice of the Holy Spirit speaking clearly to us. Maybe this is because in the evening we have no place to go but to sleep.

Regardless of when we pray and whatever may be our prayer agenda, the primary principle guiding our life of prayer is simply that God's will be done.

Prayer is medicine for the soul! Just as we often take medicine before meals, generally speaking, it is better to pray before, rather than immediately after meals. After eating, the flow of the blood is directed to the stomach to aid digestion, rather than to the brain. Thus, the mind may become drowsy. We have often noticed how difficult it is to concentrate immediately following a meal. Many schoolteachers dread the class right after lunch for that very reason. On the other hand, setting aside a time of prayer before our meals, in addition to offering our gratitude for food at meal times, may be relaxing and aid in digestion.

Generally speaking, most people under most circumstances will find morning and evening prayer times helpful in establishing the practice of regular prayer. Brief intermittent prayers, which are often prompted out of personal need, are also vital and important. These prayers seem to work better for us if we have the habit of regular prayers. If we have been meeting with God in prayer as a fixed practice, then when we have crisis occasions, where we must pray on the run, we will feel more like a regular guest in our conversation with God.

In addition to a scheduled time for our regular prayer, there are those opportune moments when riding on an airplane or bus, waiting for an appointment in a reception office, or taking a leisure walk, when we have a chance to make a connection with the Almighty. These are times when we may have short but meaningful dialogues with God.

Another great aid in helping our concentration during prayer is fasting. We have often heard about "prayer and fasting." It is the practice of many deeply religious people. The prophets in the Old Testament often fasted for lengthy periods. Jesus "fasted forty days and forty nights" (Matt. 4:2) before he had his struggle with Satan, who tempted him to surrender his divine intentions.

To "fast" means to abstain from eating. The early Christian church leaders advocated the practice of abstinence from food on special occasions. It helped their minds to move from thoughts of the flesh to be instead centered on God. It is practiced today by those who have a driving passion for certain things to happen. Many feel that going without food is the outward sign of a real inner commitment. For them it is a declaration of sacrifice and dedication. It is usually accompanied by deep prayer and is not merely a symbol of self-denial or a show of piety. For the beginner, it is generally wise to start with small fasting periods.

Systematic research suggests that fasting may have both psychological and spiritual benefits, including relief of depressed moods, improvement in decision-making ability, heightened ability to communicate with God and meditate, feeling closer to other church members and church leaders, and even some reports of physical cures.[1] Nevertheless, care must be taken during fasting by those with health issues to ensure that no problems result, due either to medication taken for illnesses or the effects of illness itself. For example, diabetics must be careful when fasting so that their blood sugars don't fall too low, especially if insulin or oral medications are taken. Fasting can also be associated with worsening of headaches and increased irritability as the length of the fast increases. Thus, while fasting may be a powerful tool for enhancing our prayer lives, it must be done with some common sense as well.

Willpower and Prayer

We began this chapter with the statement that "whatever gets our attention, gets us." We have traced the importance of focusing our attention in all areas of life. We have highlighted the when, how, and where of prayer. This information will be helpful in maximizing your prayer experience. All of this, however, only becomes real when we have a desire to pray and follow through on this desire. The part of us that makes this happen is called the will. This matter of the will is significant to all areas of life. The physician knows that a patient's willpower may be key in the healing process. Diet, exercise, and proper rest all depend on the power of the will to make them happen. In addition to enabling us to live a healthy lifestyle that prevents disease, willpower is also important in helping us recover from illnesses or accidents. A person who has been in a disabling accident or suffered a paralyzing stroke must exert tremendous effort and willpower during rehabilitation to regain or compensate for physical functions that have been lost. Willpower is essential in enabling us to steer our lives in a healthy direction.

Willpower is also basic to prayer. We must will to pray and we must will to follow up on what we learn during prayer. We may have knowledge about prayer but that is not enough. We must move beyond intention to practice.

Many times our own will, that power within to make us act, is the difference in our godly walk. St. Augustine apparently understood this when he said, "Lord, give me chastity" but then added, "not yet." The desire to do good only becomes reality when we *will* to do it. In the matter of prayer, we may want to focus on God, but it takes our willpower to get this started. We should integrate the driving forces of our lives around someone—God. We must be consumed by the majesty of God with whom we commune in prayer. Tennyson said:

> Our wills are ours, we know not how,
> Our wills are ours, to make them thine.

Having focused our attention on God when we pray, having used all the prayer helpers to make prayer a meaningful experience, and having set our will to pray regularly and to follow what prayer brings to our lives, we are left with one initiative: "Let's pray!"

And remember:

> God may not be impressed with the length of our prayers,
>   How many they are—
> The rhetoric of our prayers,
>   How beautiful they are—
> He may not notice the style of our prayers,
>   How orderly they are—
> But he will notice the heart of our prayers,
>   How sincere they are.

11

ORGANIZING OUR PRAYERS

Although prayer does not depend entirely on us, and has its ultimate source in God, successful prayer is not haphazard. Prayer has an organization and a plan. Having some structure during prayer simplifies the experience. All of us recognize the value of routine and order. Our daily lives depend on it. To succeed at work, we need a plan. In sports we "get back to the basics." In the arts, we refer to the importance of organization as form and style.

The human body also has definite order, structure, and arrangement. We depend on all of the different parts of our bodies performing in an orderly and consistent manner. When they don't, then this is called disease. For example, when the normal replication of cells becomes altered, this may develop into cancer. If the arteries in our hearts become clogged, then the normal, orderly flow of blood cannot continue to bring oxygen and nourishment to the heart muscle and we experience a heart attack. Order and structure are crucial for our continued bodily existence here on earth.

Since order and organization are so important to every area of our lives, it seems only natural that organization will improve our prayer lives. Since prayer is a conversation with God, a structure for our prayers will make our conversation easier and more familiar each time we converse.

Before discussing the organization or structure of prayer, we remind ourselves that the way in which we organize our prayers is secondary to the spirit and integrity of our prayers. Conversation among humans will vary, so will our prayers.

A prayer plan should not become merely routine or stifle the spontaneity in our conversation with God. Prayer is sometimes practiced in crises. Time and circumstances may not allow for structure. Like the story of the man who was out to sea when a storm blew up. In a tiny rubber boat he cried out, "O God, save me. The sea is so wide and this boat is so small." We all have these crisis experiences. In those moments the organization of prayer may be of little importance. Furthermore, if prayer becomes too routine and rigid in its organization, this can inhibit its life and vitality and especially its intimacy. We should seek to strike a balance between organization and intimacy. Nevertheless, when we develop a prayer routine, organizing the flow of our prayer time can make it more effective.

After we prepare ourselves, body, mind, and spirit as suggested earlier in this book, the conversation with God can move in steps that are psychologically and spiritually sound. These steps, developed over the centuries, give prayer a logical order.

Adoration and Praise

The first step in our conversation is best taken with words of *adoration* and *praise*. This sets the mood for all to follow. During these early moments, we reflect upon who God is. Our minds think about his majesty and love. We think about God being perfectly holy, without beginning or ending, all-powerful, all-pervasive, beyond all space and time, and yet still deeply personal, full of grace and compassion.

We picture God as the awesome Creator of everything, yet the tender Shepherd of us all. We acknowledge him as the supreme and mighty sovereign, yet the one who is concerned with the lilies of the field, the birds of the air, and the hairs on our head. We affirm that he set in motion the spinning of the universe, yet he breathed his own breath into his creature—humanity. By the very act of prayer, we believe that this awesome God is a Person and is approachable. Our spirit within us sings, "Holy, Holy, Holy, Lord God Almighty."

We reflect upon how he demonstrates his wisdom and his laws at work in his cosmos. We witness to his love by acknowledging the very incarnation of himself in Jesus Christ our Lord and Savior. This attitude of adoration and praise captures our attention. We quietly think about all his attributes made known to us. Doing this moves our attention away from our busy and limited world to God's presence. This is the first level of prayer—setting the mood.

We all know the importance of mood in a conversation with another human. Our attitudes and the atmosphere in which we pray have a great deal to do with what follows. This shouldn't be much of a surprise. Imagine what you do when you are trying to impress someone who is important to you. You may set a beautiful table with candles and special china and silverware, and prepare a wonderful meal, or you may invite that person to dine with you at a special restaurant where the mood is just right. You want to get that person's attention and make the experience pleasurable and enjoyable so he or she will want to spend time with you. If we do this to impress other people, should we not make the same effort to make the time we spend with God—our Creator and Lord—a special time? The more we put into making our attitudes and surroundings conducive to this experience, the more we will get out of it.

Mood is vital in prayer. Thinking about God sets the stage for us to become more receptive. We are becoming "centered" not on ourselves but on God. In prayer, we are not communing with ourselves but with God. After pondering deeply who God is, we might start our conversations like this: "Eternal God, maker of heaven and earth, I praise you for what and who you are in yourself. To me, you are sovereign; you are holy; you are my Creator, Savior, and Lord. You have my adoration and praise. I affirm that I am communicating with you now." (Sometimes it may be wise to take time here to contemplate quietly the nature of God.)

Thanksgiving

The next step in our prayer routine is thanksgiving. Having acknowledged the person and presence of God, and having expressed our praise and adoration to him, we become aware of all the wonderful gifts that have come to us from him. In thanksgiving, our concentration and focus will move from self-pity to gratitude.

A group of art students were all given a sheet of beautiful white art paper on which was one small ugly blot. The professor asked them what they saw. They all answered, "A blot." They overlooked all of the rest of the beautiful white paper and saw only the blot. Maybe the question wasn't totally fair. However, what they should have seen was the expanse of paper around the blot on which they could have designed a glorious scene. There is a tendency to focus our attention on the tiny ugly blots in our lives instead of on the great possibilities we have. We need to deliberately turn our thoughts from pity to gratitude.

Having a thankful and grateful attitude may even have physical effects on our bodies that will nourish them and promote health. Studies have shown that those who are more thankful are happier, more optimistic, have more hope, more satisfaction with life, and greater well-being and vitality.[1]

Prayer is that special time when we should move into a positive attitude of gratitude. We should take time to count our blessings. As the old gospel song written by Johnson Oatman Jr. suggests:

When upon life's billows you are tempest tossed,
When you are discouraged, thinking all is lost,
Count your many blessings, name them one by one,
And it will surprise you what the Lord hath done.

So, amid the conflict, whether great or small,
Do not be discouraged, God is over all;
Count your many blessings, angels will attend,
Help and comfort give you to your journey's end.
Count your blessings name them one by one;
Count your blessings, see what God has done.

We can list our blessings in the following categories:

- Life
- Nature
- Health
- Food
- Possessions
- Rest
- Work
- Family
- Friends
- Hope
- Faith
- Love

These blessings vary in degrees. At times in life we are healthier, have more possessions and friends. In counting our blessings it is of no value to compare our blessings with what we think others are receiving. Thanksgiving is not about competition. That attitude will block your prayers right from the start. Rejoice for what God has given others; zero in on what he has given you and let that attitude of gratitude be at the root of your prayers. Many prayers are answered right at the point of thanksgiving. This is especially true for someone suffering from depression, doubts, or loneliness. The depressed person is lifted above his thoughts of failure and emptiness as he recalls what God has done in his life. This will open the door for more blessings to come. As the lonely person offers prayers of thanks, he becomes more aware of the God who loves and gives all. As we share our gratitude for all we have received, it is an excellent time to think about God's love for us. Remember the simple but profound truth: God loves you!

Think about that. This one thought alone may lift your prayers to higher ground. God's love for each of us is profoundly personal and includes all of us, our entire being—both the good and the bad parts—at any one point in time.

We cannot fathom how inclusive is God's love for us. It goes beyond our imagination. We cannot comprehend it. It has been said that if all the water in the oceans, seas, lakes, rivers, and streams were ink; if the whole sky were a writing pad and if every human being had a writing instrument, we could not fully write the length, depth, height, or breadth of God's love.

God's love is awesome! Surround your prayers of thanksgiving, in which you name your personal blessings, with the affirming love of God directly accessible to you.

After filling your thoughts with gratitude, you may wish to say something like this: "O Lord, my God, I thank you for life and all that supports it. I am grateful for my body with which to perform the physical activities of life." (If you are handicapped or ill, thank God for your body just as it is, and become aware of the many parts of it that are still working well to provide you with life.) Thank him for a mind with which to think. (If your mind is troubled or distressed, thank him for the mind that you have and the great potential for healing that it possesses.) Thank him for your salvation in Christ. (If you are not a believer in Jesus Christ as your personal Savior, this would be a good place and time to accept him by faith.)

Then you could pray, "Lord, I thank you for all these benefits of my body, my mind, and my spirit. I thank you that you made me just as I am. I accept myself through your grace. Now,

I want to thank you for the special abilities and gifts that you have given me, and for the many people and material possessions that you have allowed to come into my life." (Here, name your blessings one by one.)

Confession

Having recalled, in our prayers of adoration and praise, who God is and how we relate to him, and having acknowledged our gratitude and thanksgiving for what he has done for us, we become sensitive to how we have missed the mark and how far we must go to become more like him. This becomes our target: to become more like God with whom we commune in prayer. As the gospel song suggests, this target is "so wide we can't get around it, so deep we can't get under it, and so high we can't get over it; we must come in at the door." Confession is the great door into God's grace.

It has been said that confession is good for the soul. Mental health practitioners have discovered that release and health may come to a patient if he or she can talk it out. This is the basis for all counseling and psychotherapy. When we confess our errors and problems to another person, this helps clear our minds if we are troubled. It helps us feel less alone and less entangled in our worries and oppression if we can share them with someone else. We don't need to carry around guilt. If we humbly and sincerely confess to God and pledge to a new course of action, this clears out the guilt, removes the spiritual haze that separates us from God, and enables us to feel joy and peace again.

Prayer is a great method for confessing our sins. Confession is not self-flagellation but an honest statement of where we stand in the chart of right and wrong. Our self-lashing won't forgive or release us. God does that through his grace. We need to talk these things out with God and not be afraid of the consequences.

In prayer, guilt is brought out into the open. It is not hidden, covered up, or in a closet, where it can spread its poison into the subconscious. We have control of our confessional process. We must believe it is necessary and have the courage to do it. We will not have inner peace and power without confession. Like thanksgiving, our prayer of confession should be specific. We should enumerate our trespasses and name them one by one:

- Sharp judgment
- Jealousy
- Cowardice
- Dark habit
- Moral failure
- Ethical weakness
- Lack of concern
- Neglected opportunities
- Other areas where we have missed the mark

As historic prayer books have summarized: "Forgive those things which we ought *not* to have done and forgive us our failure to do those things which we *ought* to have done." As we openly confess, we are assured that God will forgive our sins. This assurance runs consistently through the Bible and has been a major tenet in the Christian belief system throughout history.

As a part of the confession of our sins, we must also bring the sincere desire and willingness to repent. To repent means to turn about face. In our prayers of confession we acknowledge that we have been going in the wrong direction. In repentance we turn around, through God's grace, to move in the right direction.

These are rich moments in our prayer life. We experience cleansing, renewal, and purpose. The prayer of confession turns our prayer into resolve and faith. A prayer of confession may say something like this: "Gracious Father, as I honestly face myself, I am aware of my shortcomings, mistakes, and sins. These I confess to you. [Here make an honest recital of your specific sins.] In the light of your grace, I know I am forgiven. With your help, I turn to a new direction, and through your Holy Spirit within me, I will walk in the light of your guidance."

Supplication

Having confessed our sin and repented and turned about-face, we ask the Holy Spirit to intercede for us that we may be strengthened to move forward in Christ. To supplicate means to implore and ask for help in earnest. We acknowledge that we cannot make it alone and we ask God, in his divine power, to take us over and remake us according to his will. We pray that our lesser self, our baser nature, will be dominated by his gracious design. In these moments of our prayer we wait quietly for the Holy Spirit to assure us that he is present and will strengthen us. Our prayer of supplication may go something like this: "Loving Father and God, I am dependent upon you. Without your grace and guidance, I cannot make it. But with you, I will. Where I am weak, help me to be strong. Where I am anxious, help me to find peace. Where I am lost, help me to find direction. I put my total self into your hands."

Petition

After we have acknowledged the sovereignty of God, after we have enumerated our blessings and affirmed God's love for us, after we have confessed our sins and earnestly repented, after we have sought God to direct our lives, then we are ready to make our petitions to him. Petition means to ask for, to make our request known to God. He knows these requests before we ask, but somehow in our asking, we find our answers. By asking, we humbly acknowledge that we don't have what it takes and declare that we are dependent on God for help. This makes us able to receive answers from God, because in asking we become open and expectant for a response.

To make our prayers of petition our only prayers is to limit God's power within us. Yet it is as natural for us to make our requests to God as it is for a child in the dark to ask a parent for help. However, prayer should not be like a visit to Santa Claus. It is not like a TV show where we make a wish or turn a wheel for a fortune. When we make our request known to God, we must believe that a real divine power is hearing us and will answer our requests. His answers may not always be as we had envisioned and even desired. Experience has proven that possibly the worst thing that could happen to us is for our prayers to be answered in the very form that we want them. God may lead us in ways that seem strange for us but he always leads us. God's wise answers to what we want are intended to help us learn what he wants of us. Our goal in life should be to want for ourselves what he has in his plan for our lives. For that reason, all petitionary prayer should be couched in the words: "Not as I would want, but as you will for me."

The prayer of petition can be a tricky thing. For example, we may have no right to pray for those things that would bring hardship to another. Yet we are encouraged to "cast your burden on the Lord, and He shall sustain you" (Ps. 55:22). In the New Testament we read, "Be anxious for nothing, but in everything by prayer and supplication, with thanksgiving, let your requests be made known to God" (Phil. 4:6). We are encouraged to pray for certain and specific things. Jesus said, "Whatever you ask the Father in My name He will give you. . . . Ask, and you will receive" (John 16:23–24). Asking in Jesus' name is more than just repeating "in the name of Jesus" at the end of a prayer. Rather, it is praying to bring about everything that Jesus stood for—that is praying in Jesus' name. When we pray for things that are in accord with God's will, then they will indeed be done and we will receive.

The prayer of petition is not all there is to prayer but it is a vital element. It is not selfish or unscientific to ask God for certain things. Jesus said that we should. When we make our requests, we must let God answer them—and answer them in the way that we need, not that we want. Pray until your requests make you release your own interests and leave it for God's will to be done.

Your prayer of petition may take a form like this: "Gracious God, you know all the needs of the world. The very earth is yours. You know me and my needs better than I know myself. Yet I have been instructed to bring my requests to you in prayer. I pray for the needs of my body. Help me to be healthy in my mind and my body. Right now I pray for my healing in [name your bodily needs]. I pray for my temporal needs [name your needs for shelter, income, work, etc.]. I pray for the needs of my spirit. Help me to have more faith. Help me to be kinder, more patient, and understanding. [Here name relational and other personal problems you may have.] Answer my petitions according to your holy will. When I receive your answers to my requests let my mind know it and give me the wisdom and strength to follow it."

Intercession

The next step in prayer is intercession. In this phase of our prayer we are reaching out to God for others, interceding on their behalf. We are pleading to God to meet the need of someone other than ourselves. How can this happen? We believe that as created children of God, we are connected to one another. We identify with other human beings in body, mind, and spirit. Through our senses, we communicate. We talk, listen, see, touch, and smell, and through these sensations we are able to project feelings and thoughts to others and they to us. Just as we unite our knowledge, wisdom, strength, and industry to make things happen for the collective betterment of humankind, so may we unite our faith in interceding for one another's needs and the good of humanity. This connection gives credibility to the call for national and worldwide prayers when disaster or crisis occurs. We pray together to our common God. We believe these prayers are received by God.

Christians acknowledge that the same God who created us took on human form in the person of Jesus, whom we now call Christ. He demonstrated his zeal for all humankind to be saved for eternal life. Christ binds us together. We are his body. Jesus Christ becomes the great connector for our prayers. This lifts our prayers of intercession to a level higher than our communication with one another.

In our own prayers, when we come to this point where we reach out beyond our own needs and focus on the needs of others, we are lifting ourselves to a higher level. We become nobler people. As we pray for others, our grudges fall away. Malice, bitterness, and hostility have no common ground with honest intercession. You cannot truly pray for the healing and help of others while hating them. It won't work. You will be changed as you intercede. One of the overlooked values of the prayer of intercession is the good it does for the intercessor.

The prayer of intercession lifts our social responsibility. It widens our sympathies and broadens our understanding of others. When we offer our prayer of intercession, we demonstrate our sympathy for that person. *Sympathy* comes from two words: *syn,* meaning "together," and *pathos,* meaning "suffer." When we sympathize with another person, we allow our feelings to enter into their suffering.

The prayer of intercession lifts us beyond our own petitions. It keeps us from solely focusing on ourselves and our own personal problems. It becomes an instrument of following the great design of Jesus: "Whoever desires to save his life will lose it" (Matt. 16:25). In our prayers of intercession we lose ourselves briefly as we enter the pain of another.

Scientific studies show that people who pray for others, who offer spiritual help to others, actually enhance their own emotional health when doing so. In one study,[2] investigators randomly assigned 90 adults (referred to as "agents") to pray for the needs of 406 people (referred to as "subjects"). Agents prayed for their subjects for fifteen minutes daily for twelve weeks. Each subject was prayed for by three agents. Prior to the beginning of the prayer, participants in the study (including the agents) completed measures of depression, anxiety, and self-esteem. The scores on the well-being variables improved for both the agents and subjects of prayer over the course of the twelve-week period. In another study of over five hundred medical patients, those who regularly offered spiritual help and support to others experienced less depression, greater quality of life, greater emotional growth as a result of their stressful conditions, and more spiritual growth.[3]

The prayer of intercession provides healing power for the person being prayed for. This is especially true when we are praying for someone and he or she knows we are praying. There is scientific support for this. Dr. Dale Matthews, at Georgetown University, and his colleagues examined the effects of in-person intercessory prayer on progression of symptoms in forty patients with rheumatoid arthritis.[4] Subjects who were prayed for demonstrated significant overall improvement over a twelve-month period, with sustained reductions in tender and swollen joints, self-reported pain, fatigue, and functional impairment. In this study, only those who knew or thought they were being prayed for did better.

Where possible, we should let the person for whom we are interceding know about our prayers. There is healing power in this, and we become a vital support system to that person. Our positive faith attitude somehow bolsters his or her faith.

What happens when we pray for people and they are not aware of our prayers for them? Although the research studies that have examined this phenomenon are controversial and fraught with both scientific and theological problems, a number have found that those who were completely unaware that they were being prayed for did better than those who were not receiving the intercessory prayer.[5] Such findings have been claimed as proof of the power of intercessory prayer; nevertheless, because there is no way to scientifically explain the findings, health professionals have been reluctant to accept them.

Some would suggest that this happens through ESP (extrasensory perception). Many years ago, Dr. J. B. Khine, Director of Parapsychology at Duke University and a noted authority in the field of mental telepathy, made some observations. He suggested that prayer for another person insofar as it involves communication between minds, without use of the recognized senses, may be extrasensory communication of a telepathic type. This would involve psychokinetic forces that we do not fully understand and that have not been proven by any accepted scientific study to exist. We do understand the simple principle of mental telepathy where our human minds communicate on a level beyond our senses. Who has not picked up a telephone to talk with someone we have not communicated with in a long while, only to have that person respond, "I was just thinking about you and was going to telephone you today." Pure coincidence? Maybe. Some say this is extrasensory. Maybe. But that is not what we think occurs in intercessory prayer.

Intercessory prayer is not *horizontal,* mind to mind; it is *triangular.* We pray for others, we affirm their healing in our prayers, and somehow our faith joins with their need. It is God (separate from the sender and separate from the receiver) who is the receiving and sending station in intercessory prayer. It is God who gives the healing that is requested in our prayer for another. It is not our mind power that does the healing. Rather, it is the work of God.

We have a duty to pray for one another. We are motivated out of our hope, faith, and love. This divine triangular interaction (between the person who prays, God, and the person receiving prayer) is a great part of our prayer assurance.

Many may say, "If a little prayer helps, then maybe a lot of prayers will do even better." That may be the principle behind publishing "prayer lists" and having "prayer chains" where we get the word out to many people to pray for a certain person or a specific cause. The early church did this, and we are urged to practice it. The Book of Acts, the record of the early church, recorded how the Christians applied this principle: "We will give ourselves continually to prayer" (Acts 6:4).

Many Scripture passages encourage us to pray for one another. It isn't that God is like a politician who judges the cause by the number of letters or e-mails received. The effectiveness of such intercessory prayer is not only in the quantity of prayers but in their quality and sincerity. We are convinced that our prayers for others have a positive effect in some orderly divine fashion.

Your prayer of intercession may include thoughts like these: "Gracious Father, hear my prayer as I reach out in my faith for others. Especially I pray for [here name the person or cause and the specific need]. Guide me in my prompt actions to help where I can. Where I may offer relief, counsel, or care, make me aware. Grant me the wisdom and courage to perform as your hands and feet where I can. I also pray for those outside my own relationships. I pray for the leaders of the world [here name them if you choose]."

Dedication

The last step in the structure of prayer is dedication. We begin our visit with God with adoration and praise. This is followed by thanksgiving. Then comes confession followed by our supplication. We then make our petitions for our own needs and then intercede for the needs of others. This brings us to the high climax of our prayer where we say, "My Lord and my God." This is the act of self-surrender. This is a positive act as we give ourselves over to God and release ourselves to him.

Here are some thoughts you may consider in your prayer of consecration and dedication: "O Lord my God, I make the surrender of myself to you. Take my body, mind, and spirit to be used for the work of your kingdom and to help with all humankind, wherever you direct. Hear my prayer and guide my steps through Jesus Christ my Lord. Amen."

Having prayed, now wait on the Lord. Take time to listen to God's response. Be open and ready to receive.

12

THE POWER OF PRAYING TOGETHER

*P*rayer takes on a different dimension when we pray with others. Prayer is still reaching out to God, but we reinforce our faith, we widen our horizon of needs, and we receive spiritual energy when we pray to the Lord together. Since the beginning of the church, Christians have held that praying together is a major way for believers to bond with one another and God. We call this *corporate* prayer, which means "sharing by all in a group."

We know the value of group dynamics in every area of life. It has been shown over and over again that the support we receive from and give to one another influences our physical, emotional, and spiritual health. When we pray together to God, this unites us closer to one another, perhaps more than any other human activity. In group prayer our spirits truly become bonded to each other as we call out to God together to meet our needs.

This principle of togetherness is vital in prayer. Prayer begins in the mind and spirit of the individual and moves outward to others. Corporate prayer is not a substitute for private prayer, and private prayer is not a substitute for corporate prayer. Private prayer and corporate prayer keep us spiritually alive.

Worship

Praying together is a pillar of worship. Praising, Scripture readings, preaching, and witnessing make up the general form of worship, but prayer is the glue that seals it all together. Corporate prayer is practiced in many forms, ranging from sitting in silence to standing with everyone talking at the same time. The order for corporate prayer during a service varies from congregation to congregation. Whether the worship form is liturgical or impromptu, the content of many worship service prayers consists of invocation, adoration, confession, thanksgiving, supplication, petition, intercession, and benediction. Many churches include the recitation of the Lord's Prayer. When the worshiper leaves the service, he or she generally feels renewed in spirit.

Prayer Meetings

Prayer meetings, as they were once called, are not as popular as in years past. Some say that this may be one cause for the decline of membership in so many churches. Prayer meetings are held primarily for the purpose of praying together. They usually include singing, sharing and testimonies, prayer requests, and a time for group concentration and prayer. The point has been made that the prayer meeting went out of style because it became stereotyped. That observation may be true, but it was not a valid reason for discontinuing prayer meetings. Jesus said that "where two or three are gathered together in My name, I am there in the midst of them" (Matt. 18:20).

We need Jesus in our midst, so we need to pray together with other believers.

Congregations would do well to reinstate the prayer meeting where they do not have one. The leadership should make certain that prayer is the chief purpose for the gathering. It should be at the most convenient time for the people and need not be too long. Since Jesus promised that he would attend at our prayer meetings, we must allow time for his direction.

Small Groups

Throughout the history of the church, Christians have met in small groups for prayer. In times of political unrest these small groups or "cells" have sometimes met together in "underground" conditions. Their prayer vigils have kept the church alive when governments and regimes have tried to stamp it out. The power of prayer has given purpose, power, support, and hope to each of the cell groups' members. In Communist China and many of the Muslim countries, corporate Christian prayer today continues to take place in hidden and underground locations. Threats of jail and persecution are insufficient to stop this activity that brings people closer to their God and closer to each other.

Studies are now being conducted at Johns Hopkins to study the effects of small group prayer on immune function in women with breast cancer.[1] Group prayer has been studied among patients with rheumatoid arthritis and found to be beneficial.[2] Thus, not only are there psychological, social, and spiritual benefits to corporate prayer, but there may be physical benefits as well for those with acute or chronic health conditions.

Today congregations often have small groups who meet regularly for mutual encouragement, support, and prayer. The ideal small group size is about eight to ten members. They are often called "covenant groups" because of their agreement with each other. There are many reports on how the support of these bonded friends in prayers have kept the individuals going when the way has become very tough. These prayer fellowships have had enormously enriching results for the participants. They sometimes include neighbors, fellow employees, professional colleagues, students, athletes, or entertainers. These small groups generate great spiritual energy.

The history of the church clearly evidences the power of these small groups meeting together for prayer. The great revivals and renewals that have occurred in Christianity have had their beginnings in small prayer groups. From these small prayer settings, large spiritual results occur. If you don't belong to a covenant group, find one and join it. If you cannot find one, start one yourself with a friend or two.

Family prayers are in this "small group" category. Prayer can be the bonding element in a family when everything else seems to fail. Prayer around the dining table, family devotional times, and spiritual sharing can preserve, enrich, and guide the family. Parents, children, and other family members receive blessings individually through these prayers, while the family unit overall is strengthened. In our review of the scientific literature on religion and marital relationships, we found thirty-eight studies on this subject. Over 90 percent of these studies found that spouses who come from the same religious background or practice their faith together, especially by praying, have more satisfying and more stable marriages.[3]

Prayer Partners

Having a specific person with whom you pray has spiritual value. These prayer partners often become bonded friends for life. Our prayer partners often are the ones we turn to in times of greatest need or to celebrate our greatest joys. A prayer partner frequently enables us to make vocational and relational moves beyond our own abilities.

In addition to these prayer partners we develop outside of marriage, the husband and wife who pray together have in prayer a powerful agent that cements their relationship together.

We need not always pray alone. There are times when we need to do so, when God wants his personal time with us in private. However, fellowship is spiritually energizing for us, and God knows that such fellowship is nourished by prayer together with others. Hence, we need to balance our time in prayer, doing it both together and alone.

Prayer Is Our Spiritual Lifeline

One day in Paris, the widely regarded heretic Voltaire and his friend were watching a religious procession. As the crucifix passed in front of him, the self-styled atheist lifted his hat. In great surprise his friend exclaimed, "Sir, are you reconciled to God?" Voltaire replied, "We salute, but we do not speak." His supercilious response describes many people's relationship with God. Many people seem to only salute. Because they cannot explain the world without him, they display a certain reserved awareness of God, but they have no conscious personal relationship with him. Yet it is this personal relationship with God in Christ that gives full meaning and purpose to life. It is the relationship that lasts even when all other relationships weaken or end. Prayer is what nourishes that relationship with God.

Prayer is not only a duty but a necessity. It is our spiritual lifeline. It maintains our relationship with God. No person is at his best without prayer. To ignore or disregard prayer is like going without food or sleep. Spiritual malnutrition and fatigue result without it. Prayer gives our daily lives their base and balance.

In this important subject of prayer, we have been traveling where the saints have trod. Those who have been the strongest spiritually have been people who prayed. The practice of praying is neither new nor unexplored. Long before our modern history, people were praying. Prayer is humanity's primary tie with God. Prayer rises beyond all color lines, social standings, or economic positions. It is not limited by time or place. Prayer is universal and all encompassing.

Prayer is the instrument for bringing peace within a person as well as peace among all persons. It gives to every person inward peace to meet the demands of life, and gives to all humankind the collective power to live together in peace. Peace and power, within individuals and among all groups, are possible through prayer.

The conflicts that exist within a person, causing frustration and despair, can only be resolved by God. Efforts to bring about peace through human means alone will be helpful but not complete. Only God is capable and powerful enough to give lasting peace within us. As we are lifted up by the power of God to a single purpose to do God's will, this brings peace and satisfaction. Such an experience only comes through grace and the atonement of our Lord Jesus Christ.

Similarly, the conflicts that occur within humankind can only be resolved by God. Only as the warring natures of men are brought together in the common loving nature of God, will the world find peace. As we pray together we are united in a common fellowship. Through prayer and the uniting power of Jesus Christ, all humanity will discover its true oneness. We shall know that the forces dividing us are not nearly as great as the God uniting us. As the old hymn "The Church's One Foundation" says, "True hearts everywhere shall their high communion find."

Prayer is intimate, yet it is cosmic. Prayer is immediate, yet it is eternal. Prayer is truly the divine-human encounter. Through prayer we are made well.

Horatio Spafford, after losing his family at sea, was able to write:

> When peace, like a river, attendeth my way,
> When sorrows like sea billows roll;
> Whatever my lot, Thou hast taught me to say,
> It is well, it is well with my soul.

Prayer gives us that assurance.

PRAYER RESOURCES

SCRIPTURES ON HEALING

criptures related to healing and health are listed below. (Many others are quoted in the text.)

Deuteronomy 32:39

Psalm 6:2

Psalm 103:3

Psalm 107:20

Isaiah 6:10

Isaiah 53:5

Isaiah 61:1

Jeremiah 3:22

Hosea 6:1–3

Matthew 4:23–24

Matthew 10:8

Acts 9:33–34

Acts 14:9–10

James 5:15–16

3 John 2

ANTHOLOGY OF SCRIPTURE PRAYERS

Prayers from the Bible

The following is an anthology of prayers from the Old and New Testaments in the Bible. They are arranged in order of their appearance in the Scriptures and are listed by titles of their subjects. Read them carefully. Read them often. Let these inspired words guide you in your prayer life.

Prayer as Conversation with God

Now it came to pass after these things that God tested Abraham, and said to him, "Abraham!" And he said, "Here I am."

Genesis 22:1

A Prayer of Gratitude

I will extol You, O LORD, for You have lifted me up,
And have not let my foes rejoice over me.
O LORD, my God, I cried out to You,
And You healed me.

O LORD, You brought my soul up from the grave;
You have kept me alive, that I should not go down to the pit.
. . . .
You have turned for me my mourning into dancing;
You have put off my sackcloth and clothed me with gladness,
To the end that my glory may sing praise to You and not be
   silent.
O LORD my God, I will give thanks to You forever.

Psalm 30:1–3, 11–12

Strength in Time of Trouble

In You, O Lord, I put my trust;
Let me never be ashamed;
Deliver me in Your righteousness.
Bow down Your ear to me,
Deliver me speedily;
Be my rock of refuge,
A fortress of defense to save me.
For You are my rock and my fortress;
Therefore, for Your name's sake,
Lead me and guide me.
Pull me out of the nets which they have secretly laid for me,
For You are my strength.
Into Your hand I commit my spirit;
You have redeemed me, O LORD God of truth.

Psalm 31:1–5

Prayer for Forgiveness

Have mercy upon me, O God,
According to Your lovingkindness;
According to the multitude of Your tender mercies,
Blot out my transgressions.
Wash me thoroughly from my iniquity,
And cleanse me from my sin.
. . . .

Create in me a clean heart, O God,
And renew a steadfast spirit within me.
Do not cast me away from Your presence,
And do not take Your Holy Spirit from me.
Restore to me the joy of Your salvation,
And uphold me by Your generous Spirit.
Then I will teach transgressors Your ways,
And sinners shall be converted to You.

Psalm 51:1–3, 10–13

Prayer for Help against Enemies

Be merciful to me, O God, for man would swallow me up;
Fighting all day he oppresses me.
My enemies would hound me all day,
For there are many who fight against me, O Most High.
. . . .
When I cry out to You,
Then my enemies will turn back.

Psalm 56:1–2, 9

Prayer for Help against Danger

Save me, O God!
For the waters have come up to my neck.
I sink in deep mire,
Where there is no standing;
I have come into deep waters,
Where the floods overflow me.
. . . .
Deliver me out of the mire,
And let me not sink;
Let me be delivered from those who hate me,
And out of the deep waters.
Let not the floodwater overflow me,
Nor let the deep swallow me up;
And let not the pit shut its mouth on me.

Hear me, O LORD, for Your lovingkindness is good;
Turn to me according to the multitude of Your tender mercies.
And do not hide Your face from Your servant,
For I am in trouble;
Hear me speedily.

Psalm 69:1–2, 14–17

Prayer for Priorities

O God, behold our shield,
And look upon the face of Your anointed.
For a day in Your courts is better than a thousand.
I would rather be a doorkeeper in the house of my God
Than dwell in the tents of wickedness.

Psalm 84:9–10

Prayer for Help in Temptation

LORD, I cry out to You;
Make haste to me!
Give ear to my voice when I cry out to You.
Let my prayer be set before You as incense,
The lifting of my hands as the evening sacrifice.
Set a guard, O LORD, over my mouth;
Keep watch over the door of my lips.
Do not incline my heart to do any evil thing,
To practice wicked works
With men who work iniquity;
And do not let me eat of their delicacies.
. . . .
Let the wicked fall into their own nets,
While I escape safely.

Psalm 141:1–4, 10

Prayer of Deliverance from Death

Then Jonah prayed to the Lord his God from the fish's belly. And he said:

> "Out of the belly of Sheol I cried,
> And You heard my voice.
> For You cast me into the deep,
> Into the heart of the seas,
> And the floods surrounded me;
> All Your billows and Your waves passed over me.
> Then I said, 'I have been cast out of Your sight;
> Yet I will look again toward Your holy temple.'
> The waters surrounded me, even to my soul;
> The deep closed around me;
> Weeds were wrapped around my head.
> I went down to the moorings of the mountains;
> The earth with its bars closed behind me forever;
> Yet You have brought up my life from the pit,
> O Lord, my God."

Jonah 2:1–6

The Prayer Jesus Taught Us

In this manner, therefore, pray: Our Father in heaven, Hallowed be Your name. Your kingdom come. Your will be done on earth as it is in heaven. Give us this day our daily bread. And forgive us our debts, as we forgive our debtors. And do not lead us into temptation, but deliver us from the evil one. For Yours is the kingdom and the power and the glory forever. Amen.

Matthew 6:9–13

A Prayer for God's Will

And He said, "Abba, Father, all things are possible for You. Take this cup away from Me; nevertheless, not what I will, but what You will."

Mark 14:36

Prayer of Submission

And Mary said: "My soul magnifies the Lord, and my spirit has rejoiced in God my Savior. For He has regarded the lowly state of His maidservant; for behold, henceforth all generations will call me blessed. For He who is mighty has done great things for me, and holy is His name. And His mercy is on those who fear Him from generation to generation."

Luke 1:46–50

Prayer of Praise

And suddenly there was with the angel a multitude of the heavenly host, praising God and saying: "Glory to God in the highest, and on earth peace, goodwill toward men!"

Luke 2:13–14

A Baptismal Prayer

When all the people were baptized, it came to pass that Jesus also was baptized; and while He prayed, the heaven was opened. And the Holy Spirit descended in bodily form like a dove upon Him, and a voice came from heaven which said, "You are my beloved Son; in You I am well pleased."

Luke 3:21–22

Prayer for Forgiveness of Others

Then Jesus said, "Father, forgive them, for they do not know what they do."

Luke 23:34

Jesus Prays for Himself

Jesus spoke these words, lifted up His eyes to heaven, and said: "Father, the hour has come. Glorify Your Son, that Your Son also may glorify You, as You have given Him authority over all flesh, that He should give eternal life to as many as You have given Him. And this is eternal life, that they may know You, the only true God, and Jesus Christ whom You have sent. I have glorified You on the earth. I have finished the work which You have given Me to do. And now, O Father, glorify Me together with Yourself, with the glory which I had with You before the world was."

John 17:1–5

Jesus' Prayer for All Believers

I do not pray for these alone, but also for those who will believe in Me through their word; that they all may be one; as You, Father, are in Me, and I in You; that they also may be one in Us, that the world may believe that You sent Me. And the glory which You gave Me I have given them, that they may be one just as We are one: I in them, and You in Me; that they may be made perfect in one, and that the world may know that You have sent Me, and have loved them as You have loved Me.

Father, I desire that they also whom You gave Me may be with Me where I am, that they may behold My glory which You have given Me; for You loved Me before the foundation of the world. O righteous Father! The world has not known You, but I have known You; and these have known that You sent Me. And I declared to them Your name, and I will declare it, that the love with which You loved Me may be in them, and I in them.

John 17:20–26

Prayer of Final Commitment

And when Jesus had cried out with a loud voice, He said, "Father, 'into Your hands I commend My spirit.'"

Luke 23:46

It is finished!

John 19:30

Personal Prayer Diary

Here is your private prayer diary, with thirty numbered days for you to use consecutively or as you choose. The pages are blank, so you may use the prayer form most desirable. You may choose a structured form: (1) adoration, (2) thanksgiving, (3) confession, (4) supplication, (5) petition, (6) intercession, and (7) dedication. Or you may write in the style with which you are most comfortable. You may choose to draw a picture, create a diagram, or write a poem or story. You may wish to write a letter—"Dear God . . ."

Remember, this is more than a daily diary in which you list events of the day and resolutions for the future. The prayer diary is a record of your conversation with God. You may even choose to include some notes of what you sense God is saying to you in prayer. Hopefully these will be treasured pages for you. After these pages are filled, you may choose to continue writing some of your prayers in other tablets or notebooks.

May God bless you as you pray.

DAY ONE

_____

_____

_____

_____

_____

_____

_____

_____

_____

_____

DAY TWO

_____

_____

_____

_____

_____

_____

_____

_____

_____

_____

DAY THREE

DAY FOUR

Day Five

_____
_____
_____
_____
_____
_____
_____
_____
_____
_____
_____

Day Six

_____
_____
_____
_____
_____
_____
_____
_____
_____
_____

Day Seven

_____

_____

_____

_____

_____

_____

_____

_____

_____

_____

Day Eight

_____

_____

_____

_____

_____

_____

_____

_____

_____

_____

Day Nine

Day Ten

DAY ELEVEN

DAY TWELVE

Day Thirteen

_____

_____

_____

_____

_____

_____

_____

_____

_____

_____

Day Fourteen

_____

_____

_____

_____

_____

_____

_____

_____

_____

_____

Day Fifteen

_____

_____

_____

_____

_____

_____

_____

_____

_____

_____

Day Sixteen

_____

_____

_____

_____

_____

_____

_____

_____

_____

_____

Day Seventeen

_____

_____

_____

_____

_____

_____

_____

_____

_____

Day Eighteen

_____

_____

_____

_____

_____

_____

_____

_____

_____

DAY NINETEEN

_____
_____
_____
_____
_____
_____
_____
_____
_____
_____

DAY TWENTY

_____
_____
_____
_____
_____
_____
_____
_____
_____
_____

DAY TWENTY-ONE

_____

_____

_____

_____

_____

_____

_____

_____

_____

_____

DAY TWENTY-TWO

_____

_____

_____

_____

_____

_____

_____

_____

_____

_____

Day Twenty-Three

_____

_____

_____

_____

_____

_____

_____

_____

_____

_____

Day Twenty-Four

_____

_____

_____

_____

_____

_____

_____

_____

_____

_____

_____

Day Twenty-Five

_____

_____

_____

_____

_____

_____

_____

_____

_____

_____

Day Twenty-Six

_____

_____

_____

_____

_____

_____

_____

_____

_____

_____

DAY TWENTY-SEVEN

_____
_____
_____
_____
_____
_____
_____
_____
_____
_____

DAY TWENTY-EIGHT

_____
_____
_____
_____
_____
_____
_____
_____
_____
_____

Day Twenty-Nine

_____

_____

_____

_____

_____

_____

_____

_____

_____

Day Thirty

_____

_____

_____

_____

_____

_____

_____

_____

_____

_____

_____

NOTES

Introduction

1. Chester Tolson and Clarence William Lieb, *Peace and Power through Prayer* (Englewood Cliffs, N.J.: Prentice Hall, 1962), vii.

2. Ibid.

3. Ibid., 89.

4. Ibid.

5. Sharon Begley, "God and the Brain: How We're Wired for Spirituality," *Newsweek*, May 7, 2001, 50–51.

Chapter 1: Prayer Power

1. D. M. Johnson, J. S. Williams, and D. G. Bromley, "Religion, health, and healing: findings from a southern city," *Sociological Analysis* 47 (1986): 66–73.

Chapter 2: Stress Can Kill You

1. A. Breier, M. Albus, D. Pickar, T. P. Zahn, O. M. Wolkowitz, and S. M. Paul, "Controllable and uncontrollable stress in humans: Alterations in mood and neuroendocrine and psychophysiological function," *American Journal of Psychiatry* 144 (1987): 1419–25.

2. J. T. Cacioppo, W. B. Malarkey, J. K. Kiecolt-Glaser, B. N. Uchino, S. A. Sgoutas-Emch, J. F. Sheridan, G. G. Berntson, and R. Glaser, "Heterogeneity in neuroendocrine and immune responses to brief

psychological stressors as a function of autonomic cardiac activation," *Psychosomatic Medicine* 57 (1995): 154–64.

3. J. K. Kiecolt-Glaser, W. B. Malarkey, M. Chee, T. Newton, J. T. Cacioppo, H. Y. Mao, and R. Glaser, "Negative behavior during marital conflict is associated with immunological down-regulation," *Psychosomatic Medicine* 55 (1993): 395–409.

4. R. W. Bartrop, L. Lazarus, E. Luckhurst, L. G. Kiloh, and R. Penny, "Depressed lymphocyte function after bereavement," *Lancet* (April 16, 1977): 834–36.

5. J. Leserman, John M. Petitto, R. N. Golden, B. N. Gaynes, H. Gu, D. O. Perkins, S. G. Silva, J. D. Folds, D. L. Evans, "Impact of stressful life events, depression, social support, coping, and cortisol on progression to AIDS," *American Journal of Psychiatry* 157, no. 8 (2000): 1221–28.

6. J. K. Kiecolt-Glaser, J. R. Dura, C. E. Speicher, O. J. Trask, and R. Glaser, "Spousal caregivers of dementia victims: longitudinal changes in immunity and health," *Psychosomatic Medicine* 53 (1991): 345–62.

7. J. K. Kiecolt-Glaser, W. Garner, and C. Spelcher, "Psychosocial modifiers of immunocompetence in medical students," *Psychosomatic Medicine* 46 (1984): 7–14.

8. S. Cohen, D. A. J. Tyrell, and A. P. Smith, "Psychological stress and susceptibility to the common cold," *New England Journal of Medicine* 325 (1991): 606–12.

9. D. L. Evans, J. Leserman, D. O. Perkins, R. A. Stern, C. Murphy, B. Zheng, D. Gettes, J. A. Longmate, S. G. Silva, C. M. van der Horst, C. D. Hall, J. D. Folds, R. N. Golden, and J. M. Petitto, "Severe life stress as a predictor of early disease progression in HIV infection," *American Journal of Psychiatry* 154 (1997): 630–34.

10. S. Levy, M. Lippman, and T. d'Angelo, "Correlation of stress factors with sustained suppression of natural killer cell activity and predictive prognosis in patients with breast cancer," *Journal of Clinical Oncology* 5 (1987): 348–53.

11. S. Levy, J. Lee, C. Bagley, and G. Lippman, "Survival hazards analysis in first recurrent breast cancer patients: The seven-year follow-up," *Psychosomatic Medicine* 50 (1988): 520–28.

12. D. Roberts, B. L. Andersen, and A. Lubaroff, "Stress and immunity at cancer diagnosis" (unpublished manuscript, Ohio State University, 1994).

13. Greg Anderson, *Journeys with the Cancer Conqueror* (Kansas City: Andrews McMeel, 1999), xi.

14. J. K. Kiecolt-Glaser, P. T. Marucha, W. B. Malarkey, A. M. Mercado, and R. Glaser, "Slowing of wound healing by psychological stress," *Lancet* 346, no. 8984 (1996): 1194–96.

15. P. T. Marucha, J. K. Kiecolt-Glaser, M. Favagehi, "Mucosal wound healing is impaired by examinations stress," *Psychosomatic Medicine* 60 (1998): 362–65.

Chapter 3: Prayer Can Help Heal You

1. H. G. Koenig, H. J. Cohen, L. K. George, J. C. Hays, D. B. Larson, D. G. Blazer, "Attendance at religious services, interleukin–6, and other biological indicators of immune function in older adults," *International Journal of Psychiatry in Medicine* 27 (1997): 233–50.

2. S. Lutgendorf, "IL–6 level, stress, and spiritual support in older adults," Psychology Department, University of Iowa, Iowa City, personal communication of May 1997 cited in H. G. Koenig, M. McCullough, D. B. Larson, *Handbook of Religion and Health* (New York: Oxford University Press, 2001), 278.

3. T. E. Woods, M. H. Antoni, G. H. Ironson, and D. W. Kling, "Religiosity is associated with affective and immune status in symptomatic HIV-infected gay men," *Journal of Psychosomatic Research* 45 (1999): 165–76.

Chapter 4: What Is Prayer?

1. M. A. Schuster, B. D. Stein, L. H. Jaycox, et al., "A national survey of stress reactions after the September 11, 2001, terrorist attacks," *New England Journal of Medicine* 345 (2001): 1507–12.

Chapter 5: What Happens When We Pray?

1. S. Nolen-Hoeksema and C. Ahrens, "Age differences and similarities in the correlates of depressive symptoms," *Psychology & Aging* 17, no. 1 (2002): 116–24.

2. J. Leor, W. K. Poole, and R. A. Kloner, "Sudden cardiac death triggered by an earthquake," *New England Journal of Medicine* 334 (1996): 413–19.

3. S. R. Meisel, I. Kutz, K. I. Dayan, et al., "Effect of Iraqi missile war on incidence of acute myocardial infarction and sudden death in Israeli civilians," *Lancet* 338 (1991): 660–61.

4. L. L. Watkins and J. A. Blumenthal, "Worried to death?" *Circulation: Journal of the American Heart Association* 100 (1999): 1251.

5. R. McGee, S. Williams, and S. Nada-Raja, "Low self-esteem and hopelessness in childhood and suicidal ideation in early adulthood," *Journal of Abnormal Child Psychology* 29, no. 4 (2001): 281–91.

6. R. McGee and S. Williams, "Does low self-esteem predict health compromising behaviors among adolescents?" *Journal of Adolescence* 23, no. 5 (2000): 569–82.

7. T. Cross, C. E. Sheard, P. Garrud, T. P. Nikolopoulos, and G. M. O'Donoghue, "Impact of facial paralysis on patients with acoustic neuroma," *Laryngoscope* 110, no. 9 (2000): 1539–42.

8. D. Kirschner, "Understanding adoptees who kill: Dissociation, patricide, and the psychodynamics of adoption," *International Journal of Offender Therapy and Comparative Criminology* 36 (1992): 323–33.

9. D. E. Long, *The Anatomy of Terrorism* (New York: Free Press, 1990).

10. J. L. Craven, G. M. Rodin, L. Johnson, and S. H. Kennedy, "The diagnosis of major depression in renal dialysis patients," *Psychosomatic Medicine* 49, no. 5 (1987): 482–92.

11. M. Maes, M. Claes, M. Vandewoude, C. Schotte, M. Martin, P. Blockx, and P. Cosyns, "Adrenocorticotropin hormone, beta-endorphin and cortisol responses to oCRF in melancholic patients," *Psychological Medicine* 22, no. 2 (1992): 317–29.

12. Redford and Virginia Williams, *Anger Kills* (New York: Harper Collins, 1998).

Chapter 7: Faith and Prayer

1. Herbert Benson, *Timeless Healing: The Power and Biology of Belief* (New York: Scribner, 1996).

2. Charles S. Carver, Christina Pozo, Suzanne D. Harris, Victorial Noriega, et al., "How coping mediates the effect of optimism on distress: A study of women with early stage breast cancer," *Journal of Personality & Social Psychology* 65, no. 2 (August 1993): 375–90; Charles S. Carver, Michael F. Scheier, and Jagdish K. Weintraub, "Assessing coping strategies: A theoretically based approach," *Journal of Personality & Social Psychology* 56, no. 2 (February 1989): 267–83.

3. Hiroyasu Iso, Chigusa Date, Akio Yamamoto, Hideaki Toyoshima, Naohito Tanabe, Shogo Kikuchi, Takaaki Kondo, Yoshiyuki Watanabe, Yasuhiko Wada, Teruo Ishibashi, Hiroshi Suzuki, Akio Koizumi, Yutaka Inaba, Akiko Tamakoshi, and Yoshiyuki Ohno, "Perceived mental stress

and mortality from cardiovascular disease among Japanese men and women: The Japan Collaborative Cohort Study for Evaluation of Cancer Risk Sponsored by Monbusho (JACC Study)," *Circulation* 106, no. 10 (2002): 1229–36.

Chapter 8: The Mind and Prayer

1. Anne Underwood, "God and the Brain," *Newsweek,* May 7, 2001, 52.

2. See, for example, James Austin, *Zen and the Brain* (Cambridge, Mass.: MIT Press, 1998), and Andrew Newberg, *Why God Won't Go Away* (New York: Ballantine, 2001).

3. W. W. Surwillo and D. P. Hobson, "Brain electrical activity during prayer," *Psychological Reports* 43 (1978): 135–43.

Chapter 10: Focus and Follow-Through in Prayer

1. E. E. Griffith and G. E. Mahy, "Psychological benefits of spiritual Baptist 'mourning,'" *American Journal of Psychiatry* 141, no. 6 (1984): 769–73.

Chapter 11: Organizing Our Prayers

1. M. E. McCullough, R. A. Emmons, and J. A. Tsang, "The grateful disposition: A conceptual and empirical topography," *Journal of Personality & Social Psychology* 82, no. 1 (2002): 112–27.

2. S. O'Laoire, "An experimental study of the effects of distant, intercessory prayer on self-esteem, anxiety, and depression," *Alternative Therapies in Health and Medicine* 3, no. 6 (1997): 38–53.

3. H. G. Koenig, K. I. Pargament, and J. Nielsen, "Religious coping and health outcomes in medically ill hospitalized older adults," *Journal of Nervous and Mental Disorders* 186 (1998): 513–21.

4. D. A. Matthews, S. M. Marlowe, and F. S. MacNutt, "Effects of intercessory prayer on patients with rheumatoid arthritis," *Southern Medical Journal* 93 (2000): 1177–86.

5. R. C. Byrd, "Positive therapeutic effects of intercessory prayer in a coronary care unit population," *Southern Medical Journal* 81 (1998): 826–29; W. S. Harris, M. Bowda, J. W. Kolb, C. P. Strychacz, J. L. Vacek, P. G. Jones, A. Forker, J. H. O'Keefe, and B. D. McCallister, "The randomized, controlled trial of the effects of remote, intercessory prayer on outcomes in patients admitted to the coronary care unit," *Archives*

of Internal Medicine 159 (1999): 2273–78; K. Y. Cha, D. P. Wirth, and R. A. Lobo, "Does prayer influence the success of in vitro fertilization-embryo transfer? Report of a masked, randomized trial," *Journal of Reproductive Medicine* 46, no. 9 (2001): 781–87.

Chapter 12: The Power of Praying Together

1. D. Becker, "Prayer in black women with breast cancer," a five-year randomized clinical trial (RCT) funded as part of the Johns Hopkins' Center for Alternative and Complementary Medicine, awarded by NCCAM in August 2000 (Baltimore: Johns Hopkins Center for Health Promotion).

2. D. A. Matthews, S. M. Marlowe, and F. S. MacNutt, "Effects of intercessory prayer on patients with rheumatoid arthritis," *Southern Medical Journal* 93 (2000): 1177–86.

3. Koenig, McCullough, and Larson, 278.

Rev. Chester L. Tolson, Ph.D., is an ordained minister in the Presbyterian Church (USA). Born in Los Angeles, California, he has served as a senior pastor in San Anselmo, California, Lake Oswego, Oregon, and Rancho Santa Fe, California. He served as an executive for the Presbytery of Los Angeles, as a director for an appeal to raise mission funds for the Presbyterian General Assembly, and as the assistant to the president for Trinity University in San Antonio, Texas. For over twelve years, Tolson served as the assistant to Dr. Robert H. Schuller of the Crystal Cathedral Ministries. He is now the executive director of Churches Uniting in Global Mission (C.U.G.M.), a network of churches across all denominations and traditional lines. He lives in Apple Valley, California.

Harold Koenig, M.D., is associate professor of psychiatry and associate professor of medicine at Duke University. He is the founder and director of the Center for the Study of Religion/Spirituality and Health at Duke and has written extensively on mental health, geriatrics, and religion. Koenig is board certified in geriatric psychiatry and geriatric medicine. He is the editor of *International Journal of Psychiatry in Medicine,* a medical research journal, and the founder and editor in chief of *Research News & Opportunities in Science and Theology,* a monthly international newspaper stimulating research, education, and dialogue in science and theology. Koenig is the author of *The Healing Power of Faith* and lives in Durham, North Carolina.